T0247870

How the Brain Works

The Editors of *Scientific American*

SCIENTIFIC | EDUCATIONAL
AMERICAN | PUBLISHING

New York

Published in 2025 by **Scientific American Educational Publishing**
in association with **The Rosen Publishing Group**
2544 Clinton Street, Buffalo NY 14224

Contains material from Scientific American®, a division of Springer Nature America, Inc.,
reprinted by permission, as well as original material from The Rosen Publishing Group®.

First Edition

Scientific American
Lisa Pallatroni: Project Editor

Rosen Publishing
Michael Hessel-Mial: Compiling Editor
Michael Moy: Senior Graphic Designer

Cataloging-in-Publication Data
Names: Scientific American, inc., editor.
Title: How the brain works / the editors of Scientific American.
Other titles: How the brain works (Scientific American)
Description: First edition. | New York : Scientific American Educational
Publishing, 2025. | Series: Scientific American explores big ideas |
Includes bibliographical references and index. | Audience: Grades 10-12 |
Identifiers: LCCN 2024012816 | ISBN 9781725351783 (library binding) |
ISBN 9781725351776 (paperback) | ISBN 9781725351790 (ebook)
Subjects: LCSH: Brain–Juvenile literature. | Brain–Physiology–Juvenile literature.
Classification: LCC QP376 .H7577 2025 | DDC 612.8/2–dc23/eng/20240503
LC record available at https://lccn.loc.gov/2024012816

Manufactured in the United States of America
Websites listed were live at the time of publication.

Cover: SpeedKingz/Shutterstock.com

CPSIA Compliance Information: Batch # CSSA25.
For Further Information contact Rosen Publishing at 1-800-237-9932.

CONTENTS

Introduction   6

Section 1: Brain Cells   7

1.1   The Father of Modern Neuroscience Discovered the Basic
Unit of the Nervous System   8
By Benjamin Ehrlich

1.2   The Hidden Brain   15
By R. Douglas Fields

1.3   Newfound Hybrid Brain Cells Send Signals like
Neurons Do   26
By Simon Makin

Section 2: Memory and Learning   28

2.1   A Challenge to the Textbooks on How We Learn about Our
Surroundings   29
By Gary Stix

2.2   Emotion Selectively Distorts Our Recollections   34
By Ingfei Chen

2.3   Deeper Insights Emerge into How Memories Form   44
By R. Douglas Fields

Section 3: Techniques in Brain Research   50

3.1   Controlling the Brain with Light   51
By Karl Deisseroth

3.2   A Cell Atlas Reveals the Biodiversity inside Our Head   63
By Christof Koch, Hongkui Zeng, and Ed S. Lein

3.3   "Mini Brains" Are Not like the Real Thing   70
By Karen Weintraub

3.4   The Fading Dream of the Computer Brain   74
By Noah Hutton

Section 4: The Conscious Mind 78

4.1 How Our Brain Preserves Our Sense of Self 79
By Robert Martone

4.2 A 25-Year-Old Bet about Consciousness Has Finally
Been Settled 84
By John Horgan

4.3 Some Patients Who "Died" but Survived Report Lucid
"Near-Death Experiences," a New Study Shows 89
By Rachel Nuwer

4.4 How the Mind Emerges from the Brain's
Complex Networks 93
By Max Bertolero and Dani S. Bassett

Section 5: Non-Human Brains 105

5.1 What Makes Our Brains Special? 106
By Diana Kwon

5.2 Bird Brains Have as Many Neurons as Some Primates 110
By Sara Chodosh

5.3 The Genius of Pinheads: When Little Brains Rule 113
By Erik Vance

5.4 Cetaceans' Big Brains Are Linked to Their Rich
Social Life 119
By Amanda Montañez and Diana Kwon

Section 6: Treating the Brain 121

6.1 Five Types of Research, Underexplored until Recently,
Could Produce Alzheimer's Treatments 122
By Kenneth S. Kosik

6.2 New Research Points to Causes for Brain Disorders
with No Obvious Injury 133
By Z Paige L'Erario

6.3 Forgotten Memories of Traumatic Events Get Some
Backing from Brain-Imaging Studies 138
By Joshua Kendall

6.4 The Invisible Victims of Traumatic Brain Injury 143
By Anne P. DePrince and Kim Gorgens

6.5 Elon Musk's Secretive Brain Tech Company Debuts a
    Sophisticated Neural Implant   146
    By Tanya Lewis and Gary Stix
6.6 New Brain Implant Turns Visualized Letters into Text   151
    By Bret Stetka

Glossary   154
Further Information   156
Citations   157
Index   158

INTRODUCTION

B rains are among the most complex entities in the universe, and it feels like we're only beginning to understand them. We have many biases to overcome in order to do so. Over history we've had a tendency to compare the brain to whatever current cutting-edge technology is around: books, bellows, telegraphs, computers, and beyond. We still separate the brain from the body, and treat the human brain as superior to those of all other species. This title is intended to help overcome those biases.

Section 1, "Brain Cells," explores the variety of cells and their functions. Beginning with the discovery of neurons to the discovery of other cell types that play a role, we learn how the field has expanded. Section 2, "Memory and Learning," focuses on the brain's signature task. This section explores path-breaking understanding of myelin's role in knowledge retention and the counter-intuitive nature of memory. Section 3, "New Techniques in Brain Research," showcases advances in studying the brain, especially the novel discipline of optogenetics. Promising but sometimes-criticized methods like virtual brains and organoids are explored in their weaknesses and strengths. Section 4, "The Conscious Mind," dives into the mysterious world of the mind. What does it mean to have a self, perceive, or die? Section 5, "Non-Human Brains," is a strong reminder that the human brain isn't the only standard. We learn the power of small brains and the ways differently structured brains can resemble our own. Section 6, "Treating the Brain," closes with ways doctors respond to brain disorders and mental illness. Along with diseases such as Alzheimer's, we get a better insight into mental disorders that are harder to diagnose.

One of the pleasures of learning about the brain is that every action you take is related to it. You reading this book, breaking for a snack or exercise, and even daydreaming, is happening with the support of millions of cells, connected in marvelous ways, to share impulses with one another.

Section 1: Brain Cells

1.1   The Father of Modern Neuroscience Discovered the
Basic Unit of the Nervous System
     By Benjamin Ehrlich

1.2   The Hidden Brain
     By R. Douglas Fields

1.3   Newfound Hybrid Brain Cells Send Signals like Neurons Do
     By Simon Makin

The Father of Modern Neuroscience Discovered the Basic Unit of the Nervous System

By Benjamin Ehrlich

H our after hour, year after year, Santiago Ramón y Cajal sat alone in his home laboratory, head bowed and back hunched, his black eyes staring down the barrel of a microscope, the sole object tethering him to the outside world. His wide forehead and aquiline nose gave him the look of a distinguished, almost regal, gentleman, although the crown of his head was as bald as a monk's. He had only a crowd of glass bottles for an audience, some short and stout, some tall and thin, stopped with cork and filled with white powders and colored liquids; the other chairs, piled high with journals and textbooks, left no room for anyone else to sit. Stained with dye, ink and blood, the tablecloth was strewn with drawings of forms at once otherworldly and natural. Colorful transparent slides, mounted with slivers of nervous tissue from sacrificed animals still gummy to the touch from chemical treatments, lay scattered on the worktable.

With his left thumb and forefinger, Cajal adjusted the corners of the slide as if it were a miniature picture frame under the lens of his microscope. With his right hand, he turned the brass knob on the side of the instrument, muttering to himself as he drew the image into focus: brownish-black bodies resembling inkblots and radiating threadlike appendages set against a transparent yellow background. The wondrous landscape of the brain was finally revealed to him, more real than he could have ever imagined.

In the late 19th century most scientists believed the brain was composed of a continuous tangle of fibers as serpentine as a labyrinth. Cajal produced the first clear evidence that the brain is composed of individual cells, later termed neurons, that are fundamentally the same as those that make up the rest of the living world. He believed that neurons served as storage units for mental impressions such as thoughts and sensations, which combined to form our experience of being alive: "To know the brain is equivalent to ascertaining the material course of thought and will," he wrote. The highest ideal for a biologist, he declared, is to clarify the enigma of the self. In the structure of neurons, Cajal thought he had found the home of consciousness itself.

Cajal is considered the founder of modern neuroscience. Historians have ranked him alongside Darwin and Pasteur as one of the greatest biologists of the 19th century and among Copernicus, Galileo and Newton as one of the greatest scientists of all time. His masterpiece, *Texture of the Nervous System of Man and the Vertebrates*, is a foundational text for neuroscience, comparable to *On the Origin of Species* for evolutionary biology. Cajal was awarded the Nobel Prize in 1906 for his work on the structure of neurons, whose birth, growth, decline and death he studied with devotion and even a kind of compassion, almost as though they were human beings. "The mysterious butterflies of the soul," Cajal called them, "whose beating of wings may one day reveal to us the secrets of the mind." He produced thousands of drawings of neurons, as beautiful as they are complex, which are still printed in neuroanatomy textbooks and exhibited in art museums. More than 100 years after he received his Nobel Prize, we are indebted to Cajal for our knowledge of what the nervous system looks like. Some scientists even have Cajal's drawings of neurons tattooed on their bodies. "Only true artists are attracted to science," he said.

A New Truth

In Cajal's day, the most advanced method for visualizing cells was histology, an intricate and temperamental process of staining dissected tissue with chemicals whose molecules clung to the subtle architecture of the cells, rendering them miraculously visible through a light microscope. With the primitive stains available, researchers across Europe tried and failed to clarify the question of what lies inside the brain, believed to be the organ of the mind. Then, in 1873, in the kitchen of his apartment in Abbiategrasso, outside Milan, Italian researcher Camillo Golgi, through some combination of luck and skill, hit on a new technique that revolutionized neuroanatomy. "I have obtained magnificent results and hope to do even better in the future," Golgi wrote in a letter to a friend, touting his method as so powerful that it could reveal the structure of nervous tissue "even to the blind." He called it the black reaction. One of Golgi's students recognized "the marvelous beauty of the black reaction ... [which] allows even the layman to appreciate the images in which the cell silhouette stands out as if it had been drawn by Leonardo." Cajal, who first saw the technique in the home of a colleague who had recently returned from studying in Paris, was absolutely smitten. "On the perfectly translucent yellow background," Cajal recalled, "sparse black filaments appeared that were smooth and thin or thorny and thick, as well as black triangular stellate or fusiform bodies! One would have thought that they were designs in Chinese ink on transparent Japanese paper ... Here everything was simple, clear, and unconfused ... The amazed eye could not be removed from this contemplation. The dream technique is a reality!"

Although the black reaction dramatically reduced the number of nerve elements visible on a microscope slide, those elements were still so densely packed that their fibers appeared inextricable from one another. Traditionally, researchers studied nervous tissue from adult humans who had died naturally after a normal life span. The problem was that in the adult nervous system, the fibers were already fully grown and therefore extremely structurally complex. Looking for a solution to this problem, Cajal turned to embryology—also known as ontogeny—which he had first read about in a college textbook. "If we view the natural sequence in reverse," Cajal explained, "we should hardly be surprised to find that many structural complexities of the nervous system gradually disappear." In the nervous systems of younger specimens, cell bodies would in theory be simpler, fibers shorter and less numerous, and the relationships among them easier to discern. The nervous system was also well suited to the embryological method because as axons grow, they develop myelin sheaths—insulating layers of fat and protein—which repel the silver microcrystals, preventing the enclosed fibers from being stained. Younger axons without thick sheaths more fully absorb the stain. In addition, mature axons, which sometimes grow to be a few feet long, are more likely to get chopped off during sectioning. "Since the full-grown forest turns out to be impenetrable and indefinable," he wrote, "why not revert to the study of the young wood in the nursery stage, as we might say?"

At the age of 36, Cajal found himself incubating eggs, just as he had loved doing when he was a child. This time, instead of waiting to witness "the metamorphosis of the newly born," Cajal cut into the eggshell after a few days and removed the embryo. Embryonic tissue was too delicate to withstand pressure from the clasp of a microtome. So, holding the block of tissue between the thumb and forefinger of his left hand, he cut sections with a razor blade, applying his training as a barber during the hated apprenticeships of his youth, in a fashion that he could never have foreseen. A private student of Cajal's in Barcelona who worked in the laboratory with him attested that his hand-cut sections—often between 15 and 20 microns thick—were as perfect as those cut with any machine.

In April 1888, Cajal prepared samples from the cerebellum of a three-day-old pigeon embryo. Through the microscope, he fixed his gaze on a clear, fine axon as it arced downward from its base—a soft, conical bulge on the cell body—and followed the black line, transfixed, as if he were still a boy following the course of a river. The axon curved, running alongside the layer of cells below it until it started to branch. In Cajal's eyes, the Purkinje cell stained with the black reaction resembled the "most elegant and leafy tree." He traced a branch from the cell's central "pearlike" body all the way to its end, where it approached other cells, known as stellate cells, each forming a kind of "basket" shape. Though intimately related, the "pear" of one cell and the "basket" of another never touched.

Cajal sensed a "new truth" arising in his mind: nerve cells ended freely. They were distinct individuals.

The Tangled Jungle

Since researchers first began to study the nervous system in ancient times, they have tended to compare its structure to contemporary technologies. The ancient Egyptians saw in the exterior casing of the brain, with its fissures and convolutions, the corrugated slag left over from smelting ore. The ancient Greeks thought the brain functioned like a catapult. René Descartes believed that animal spirits flowed from the brain through hollow nerves and inflated the muscles, just as hydraulic fluid traveled through machines in the royal gardens at Saint-Germain. In the 19th century, a new era of transportation, anatomist Otto Deiters, among many others, conceived of the nervous system as a railroad, with junctions at which traffic could be routed.

In the mid-19th century the railway metaphor for the nervous system gave way to another transformative technological advance: the telegraph. The German biophysical school, headed by Hermann von Helmholtz and Emil du Bois-Reymond, led the charge. "The wonder of our time, electrical telegraphy, was long ago modeled in the animal," du Bois-Reymond said in an 1851 speech. He argued that the similarity between the nervous system and the electrical telegraph ran far deeper. "It is more than similarity," he wrote. "It is a kinship between the two, an agreement not merely of the effects, but also perhaps of the causes." In turn, engineers who designed telegraph networks, such as Samuel Morse and Werner von Siemens, looked to the biological nervous system as a model of centralization and organization. With people traveling across countries for the first time and communicating with one another across the world, interconnectedness became a social ideal. When Germany finally unified in 1871, its telegraph network, centered in Berlin and reaching all its territories, became both a symbol and an instrument of imperial power. Around that time, perhaps influenced by the predominant metaphor, German anatomist Joseph von Gerlach looked at nervous tissue through his microscope and saw the tangle of fibers—a reticulum.

Cajal, who grew up in the preindustrial countryside, saw in the nervous system the natural images of his childhood. "Is there in our parks any tree more elegant and leafy than the Purkinje corpuscle of the cerebellum or the psychic cell, in other words, the famous cerebral pyramid?" he asked. He observed branchlets of axons "in the manner of moss or brambles on a wall," oftentimes supported by "a short, delicate stem like a flower"; a year later he settled on the term "mossy fibers." These fibers, he found, end in "rosettes" that approach the dendrites of other cells but, again, do not touch them. There are "nest endings" and "climbing fibers," which cling "like ivy or vines to the trunk of a tree."

Above all, the cells seemed to connect like "a forest of outstretched trees." Gray matter was an "orchard"; pyramidal cells were packed into an "inextricable grove." Cajal hit on the embryological method for studying the nervous system, he said, while reflecting on the difference in complexity between the "full-grown forest" and the "young wood." The cerebral cortex, impenetrable and wild, was a "terrifying jungle," as intimidating as the one in Cuba, where he had fought in the Ten Years' War. By force of will, Cajal believed, human beings can transform "the tangled jungle of nerve cells" into "an orderly and delightful garden." Cajal always feared that the backwardness of his environment had stunted his intellectual growth. "I regret that I did not first see the light in a great city," he wrote in his autobiography. But the undeveloped landscape of his childhood became the rich ground that nourished an understanding that was distinct from that of his contemporaries.

Although he evoked the telegraph from time to time, in an address written by him and read in his absence at the 1894 International Medical Congress in Rome, Cajal fundamentally rejected the metaphor. His opposition was rooted in both his anatomical findings and his observations of his own mind. "A continuous preestablished net—like the lattice of telegraphic wires in which no new stations or new lines can be created—somehow rigid, immutable, incapable of being modified," he said, "goes against the concept that we all hold of the organ of thought: that within certain limits, it is malleable and capable of being perfected by means of well-directed mental gymnastics." He knew, in other words, that he could change his own mind. That was why he could not tolerate the reticulum, whose structure was fixed. The nervous system must have the capacity to change, and that capacity, he argued, is crucial to an organism's survival. Cajal relied on a variety of terms to express this concept: "dynamism," "force of internal differentiation," "adaptation [of neurons] to the conditions of the environment"—and, most consequentially, "plasticity."

Cajal was not the first to use the term "plasticity," although his Rome address, delivered before a broad international audience, was probably responsible for its popularization. The concept remains one of Cajal's most enduring contributions to science, inspired by his unique and unconventional worldview.

About the Author

Benjamin Ehrlich is author of The Dreams of Santiago Ramón y Cajal, *the first English translation of Cajal's dream journals. His work has appeared in the* New England Review, Nautilus *and the* Paris Review Daily. *His new book is* The Brain in Search of Itself *(Farrar, Straus and Giroux, 2022).*

The Hidden Brain

By R. Douglas Fields

S itting in a darkened lab at the National Institutes of Health in 1999, my colleague Beth Stevens and I prepared to send a mild electric current through fetal mouse neurons in a cell culture. We were using a new microscope technique that would let us see electrical activity as a bright fluorescence emitted from a dye we had added to the culture, and we were hoping to find out if another kind of cell common in the nervous system would react in some way—Schwann cells, odd-looking cells that fabricate insulation around neurons. We didn't really expect them to; Schwann cells cannot communicate electrically. I flipped the switch. The neurons immediately glowed. But then the Schwann cells began to glow as well. It was as if they were talking back.

The most mysterious substance on Earth is the stuff between your ears, and much of the intrigue exists because many long-held beliefs about how the brain works have turned out to be wrong. Like medieval astronomers who were shocked to learn that the Earth is not the center of the universe, neuroscientists today are facing a similar revelation about neurons.

Until recently, our understanding of the brain was based on a century-old idea called the neuron doctrine. This theory holds that all information in the nervous system is transmitted by electrical impulses over networks of neurons linked through synaptic connections. But this bedrock theorem is deeply flawed. New research proves that some information bypasses the neurons completely, flowing without electricity through networks of cells called glia. The studies are upending our understanding of every aspect of brain function in health and disease, bringing answers to long-standing riddles about how we remember and learn.

Glial cells interact with neurons, control them, work alongside them—and the functions of these strange-looking cells are myriad. Star-shaped astrocytes ferry neurotransmitters, food and waste. Cephalopodlike oligodendrocytes and sausage-shaped Schwann cells wrap themselves around neurons like sheaths, speeding their electrical transmissions and helping control muscle contractions throughout the body. Microglia, ranging in form from multibranch to ameboid, are the brain's first responders to injury and disease, killing invading germ cells and beginning the process of repair.

Especially exciting is new research showing the central role of glia in information processing, neurological disorders and psychiatric illness. Some glial cells speed information between distant regions of the brain, helping us master complex cognitive processes. Others break down as they age and in their failure bring dementia. This research has great implications not only for understanding how the brain works but also for developing new treatments for neurological and psychological illnesses.

And all this comes down to a class of brain cells dismissed for 100 years as mere putty. In the 19th century, when pioneering scientists first trained microscopes on gray matter, they were amazed to find a cell unlike any other in the body: the neuron. At one end of this dazzling cell was a long, wirelike structure called the axon that carried electrical impulses to a cluster of transmission terminals. At the opposite end, the neuron sprouted busy, rootlike dendrites that received signals from the axons of other neurons, ferried across the space that separated them—the synapse—by tailor-made chemicals. Neurons were scattered sparsely throughout the brain like juicy raisins, but few cared to examine the seemingly bland dough in which they were embedded.

But, as Sherlock Holmes observed, "There is nothing more deceptive than an obvious fact," and the fact that scientists were ignoring is that neurons make up only 15 percent of our brain cells; the other 85 percent were considered little more than packing material. Indeed, 19th-century German pathologist Rudolf Virchow, one of the first to study glia, likened this brain matter to connective tissue and dubbed it *nervenkitt*, meaning nerve putty or cement, which in English became "neuroglia," from the Greek root for glue.

Few scientists are drawn to brain research to study glue. We still have no singular noun equivalent to neuron when we speak about an individual glial cell. Virchow barely distinguished between the different sorts of glia. And none of this mishmash of bizarre-looking cells had any of the telltale features essential for neuronal communication, such as axons, dendrites or synapses, so scientists had no reason to suspect that glia might be communicating in secret and doing so in an unexpected way.

A Language of Their Own

Neurons use both electricity and chemistry to convey information, with electricity transmitting impulses along the wirelike axon and chemicals carrying those signals across the synapse to another neuron. The recipient neuron then fires an electrical impulse and relays the signal to the next neuron in the chain.

Only in the past few years have scientists come to realize that the glial cells called astrocytes can control synaptic communication. So named because early anatomists thought they resembled stars, astrocytes were at first thought to be responsible only for housekeeping functions such as transporting nutrients from the bloodstream to the neurons and carrying waste in the opposite direction. These functions were surmised from the way many astrocytes cling to blood vessels with some of their arms and reach deep into brain tissue with others, tightly grasping neurons and their synapses. Only later did scientists come to see that neurons are utterly dependent on glia to fire their electrical impulses and to pass messages to one another across synapses. A clue that this dependency might be the case was the discovery of the same neurotransmitter receptors on glia as on neurons. As it happens, glia were listening to neurons and talking among themselves without using electricity at all.

This discovery awaited the invention of new tools allowing electrical activity to be seen as flashes of light. The microelectrodes that neuroscientists typically use to probe neuronal function are deaf to glial communication. But video and laser-illuminated microscopes developed in the 1980s and 1990s let researchers monitor neuronal firing by adding tracer dyes to the cells. Like the fluorescent fluid in a glow stick, these dyes shone when ions such as calcium entered neurons as their axons carried a signal, causing the dye to generate light. Very quickly those of us using these new methods saw that when we stimulated a neuron to fire an impulse, the neuroglia, hidden in plain sight, flashed back. Glia had sensed the electrical activity in neurons, and somehow calcium ions had flooded into them as well, producing the same green glow.

The new technique also revealed that glia communicate with one another in the same way. Scientists observed that when neurotransmitters released by neurons stimulated receptors on glia, the glia released neurotransmitters as well. And the release stimulated a chain reaction as the message was passed to other glia. The glial communication is stunningly evident as a wave of fluorescent light sweeping from one glial cell to the next after a neuron has fired and released a neurotransmitter.

This finding led to a bigger question: whether glial networks use the information gleaned about neuronal communication at a synapse to manage neuronal signaling at synapses in distant parts of the brain. If so, glia might have a central part in information processing itself.

Recent research provides tantalizing evidence of such a role. Using a laser to stimulate a calcium wave in an astrocyte next to an axon, a team led by neurobiologist Norio Matsuki of the University of Tokyo reported earlier this year that neurotransmitters released from the astrocyte boosted the strength of an electrical impulse in the axon. A 2005 study led by neurobiologist Philip Haydon, now at Tufts University, showed that astrocytes provide a nonelectrical pathway for communication between synapses in a brain area governing memory, the hippocampus. After responding to the neurotransmitter glutamate released from one synapse, astrocytes released a different neurotransmitter, adenosine, affecting the strength not only of its neuronal neighbor but of distant synapses as well. By controlling data processing at synapses, glia participate in aspects of vision, memory, muscle contraction and unconscious brain functions such as sleep and thirst.

The pace and breadth of glial communication provide another bit of evidence that glia play a part in information processing. Unlike neurons, which communicate serially across chains of synapses, glia broadcast their signals widely, like cell phones. Neurons' electrical communication is quite rapid, zipping through neural networks in mere thousandths of a second, but the chemical communication of glia is very slow, spreading as a tidal wave through neural tissue at a pace of seconds or tens of seconds. Rapid response is critical for certain functions—reflexive recoil from a pain stimulus, for example—but many important processes in the brain occur over longer periods.

Not the least important of these is learning. New human brain-imaging techniques have revealed that after learning to play a musical instrument or to read or to juggle, structural changes occur in brain areas that control these cognitive functions. Remarkably the changes are seen in regions where there are no complete neurons: the "white matter" areas, formed from bundles of axons coated with myelin, a white electrical insulator. Previously all theories of learning held that we incorporate new information solely by strengthening synaptic connections, but there are few synapses in white matter. Clearly, something else is happening.

Findings from my lab in the past 10 years concern two different types of glial cells that cling to axons and coat them with myelin insulation—oligodendrocytes in the brain and Schwann cells in the body. Like an octopus, each cellular tentacle of an oligodendrocyte cell grips an individual segment of an axon and wraps up to 150 layers of compacted cell membrane around it in the way an electrician wraps tape around a wire. This insulation changes how impulses travel through axons, increasing the transmission speed by up to 50 times.

And much like astrocytes at synapses, these myelin-forming glia could sense the impulses transmitted through axons. This capability was a puzzle at first, because such glia are far from the synapses where neurotransmitters are released. But my lab recently discovered that axons also release neurotransmitters through channels in their membrane that open when the axon fires. I was able to see the release of one such neurotransmitter—adenosine triphosphate, or ATP— by fitting my microscope with an extremely high-gain night-scope image intensifier that can detect single photons. For my experiment, I exploited the chemical reaction that produces a firefly's telltale green flash. I took the protein and enzyme from the tail of a firefly and added them to cultures containing mouse neurons. The firefly proteins require one more ingredient before they can glow: ATP, normally supplied by firefly cells. When I stimulated the mouse axons with a mild electric shock, they released ATP, eliciting a burst of photons.

The formation of myelin in response to stimuli likely means that early life experience plays a big role in brain development. By increasing the speed of information transfer between parts of the brain involved in mastering complex cognitive tasks, these glial cells are essential to learning, too.

How the Brain Goes Awry

Glial cells have also emerged as major actors in a host of neurological and psychological illnesses ranging from epilepsy to chronic pain to depression. Indeed, recent research has found that many neurological disorders are in fact disorders of the glia, in particular a class of cells called the microglia, which serve as the brain's defense against disease. These specialists seek out and kill invading germs and promote recovery from injury, clearing away diseased tissue and releasing powerful compounds that stimulate repair. And their function is a factor in every aspect of neurological illness.

New research suggests to some scientists that the dementia of Alzheimer's disease could be a direct outcome of microglia that have lost the ability to clear waste. Alois Alzheimer first noted that microglia surround the amyloid plaques that are the hallmark of the disease. Normally microglia digest the toxic proteins that form these plaques. But recent studies led by neuroscientist Wolfgang J. Streit of the University of Florida College of Medicine and others suggest that microglia become weaker with age and begin to degenerate. The atrophy is visible under a microscope. Senescent microglia in aged brain tissue become fragmented, losing many of their cellular branches.

The way Alzheimer's courses through the brain is one more sign of microglial involvement. Tissue damage spreads in a predetermined manner, beginning near the hippocampus and eventually reaching the frontal cortex. Streit's observations show that microglial degeneration follows the same pattern—and in advance of neuronal degeneration, suggesting that senescence of microglia is a cause of Alzheimer's dementia and not a response to neuron damage, as Alzheimer and most experts had presumed. This discovery may lead to new treatments for dementia, once researchers determine why microglia become senescent with age in some people but not in others.

The functions of the glial cells also account for why some people develop horrible chronic pain that does not relent after an injury has healed and sometimes even worsens. Doctors must use powerful narcotics such as morphine and other opiates to blunt the unrelenting pain in such patients. These drugs lose their strength over time, necessitating higher doses for the same effects, which can lead to drug dependence.

We now know that malfunctions of glial cells may account for both persistent pain and the diminishing power of some pain-relieving drugs. Research by Linda Watkins of the University of Colorado at Boulder, Kazuhide Inoue of Kyushu University in Fukuoka, Japan, and Joyce DeLeo of Dartmouth Medical School, among many others, reveals that microglia and astrocytes respond to the hyperactivity in pain circuits after injury by releasing compounds that initiate the healing process. These substances also stimulate neurons. Initially this heightened sensitivity is beneficial, because the pain forces us to protect the injury from further damage. With chronic pain, microglia do not stop releasing these substances even when healing is complete. But in recent studies pain in experimental animals was sharply reduced when the researchers blocked either the signals from neurons to glia or the signals that glia release. Scientists are now developing painkillers that target glia rather than neurons.

Glial cells also account for the ancient mystery of why spinal cord injury results in permanent paralysis. Martin Schwab of the University of Zurich and others have found that proteins in the myelin insulation that oligodendrocytes wrap around axons stop injured axons from sprouting and repairing damaged circuits. Blocking these proteins allows damaged axons to regrow in experimental animals. Clinical trials on patients with spinal cord injury are now under way.

That glia would play a central role in neurological illness is easy to understand because astrocytes and microglia are the first responders to disease. We have also long known that demyelinating disorders such as multiple sclerosis, which strips the myelin insulation from axons, cause severe disability. But it came as a recent surprise to find glia implicated in psychiatric illness. Recent work has linked chemicals called cytokines, which are released by immune system cells and microglia, to obsessive-compulsive disorder. In 2002 molecular geneticist Mario Capecchi and his colleagues in the department of human genetics at the University of Utah reported that mice with a mutation in the Hoxb8 gene exhibited compulsive grooming and hair removal behavior similar to humans with obsessive-compulsive disorder. The only cells in the brain that have this gene are microglia. Then, in a 2010 study, the researchers harvested immature immune cells that will develop into microglia from normal mice and transplanted them into the mutants. The mice were cured of their compulsive grooming behavior. Presumably cytokines released from microglia excite brain circuits responsible for habit formation.

Analysis of postmortem brain tissue has also linked oligodendrocytes and astrocytes to depression and schizophrenia by revealing reduced numbers of these cells. So have MRI examinations of people with schizophrenia, which show anomalies in subcortical white matter regions of the brain. Although psychiatric illnesses are likely to have many different causes, schizophrenia and several other mental illnesses have a strong genetic basis. If an identical twin develops schizophrenia, there is a 50–50 chance that the sibling will as well.

Some of the genes implicated in these mental illnesses are found only in oligodendrocytes; others control development of these myelin-forming glia. An analysis of 6,000 genes in tissue from the prefrontal cortex of people with schizophrenia by Yaron Hakak, then at the Genomics Institute of the Novartis Research Foundation in San Diego, revealed that 89 genes were abnormal; remarkably 35 of them are involved in myelination. Presumably these genetic abnormalities upset such processes as synaptic function and myelin insulation, which in turn could disrupt information transmission in the higher-level cognitive circuits affected in psychiatric illnesses.

Roots of Mental Illness

Investigators have set out to learn why glial cells would cause these synaptic snafus. Consider that the biological basis for most mental illness is an imbalance in neurotransmitter chemicals in circuits controlling perception, emotion and thought. All drugs used to treat mental illness and most neurological diseases work by regulating the balance of neurotransmitters. The selective serotonin reuptake inhibitors (SSRIs) used to treat chronic depression and many other psychiatric conditions work by impairing removal of serotonin and dopamine from synapses, allowing these neurotransmitters to build up and in effect boosting the signal. In a similar way, all hallucinogenic drugs, from LSD to PCP, produce their mind-bending effects by altering the levels of neurotransmitters in specific neurological circuits. Regulating neurotransmitter levels at synapses is precisely what astrocytes do.

In theory, then, astrocytes are in a position to control the balance between mental health and madness. In a strange and largely forgotten coincidence, glia were the inspiration for the revolutionary idea that mental illness could have a biological cause and that psychiatric illness could be corrected with medical treatment, albeit a very peculiar one. In the 1930s Hungarian psychopathologist Ladislas von Meduna noticed during autopsies that the number of astrocytes was abnormally low in the cerebral cortex of people who had suffered from chronic depression and schizophrenia. Von Meduna and other pathologists also knew from examination of brain tissue obtained by biopsy that the number of astrocytes increases after epilepsy, presumably to regulate electrical activity when it spins wildly out of control.

Von Meduna observed as well that people with epilepsy rarely suffered schizophrenia. He surmised that a deficiency in astrocytes was the biological reason for schizophrenia and chronic depression. By inducing a seizure in such people, he could correct the imbalance in astrocytes and cure patients suffering from these illnesses. He later wrote in his autobiography: "I published this work in 1932 without knowing that this would become the origin of shock treatment." How it works is still unclear, but electroshock therapy remains the most effective treatment for chronic depression in people who are not responsive to drugs.

The new awareness of glia in brain function suggests that drugs targeting glia might help treat mental and neurological illnesses. "Epilepsy is a prime candidate for glial-based therapeutics," says Haydon of Tufts. Recent studies by Haydon, Maiken Nedergaard of the University of Rochester Medical Center, Giorgio Carmignoto of the University of Padua in Italy, and many others are using calcium imaging and electrophysiology to show that when neuronal activity is heightened, glia release neurotransmitters that can either contribute to seizure activity or suppress it. New research also implicates glia in sleep disorders, a component of many mental illnesses. Haydon demonstrated the link in experiments on mice genetically altered to prevent their astrocytes from releasing neurotransmitters, disrupting sleep regulation.

Transformational moments are legendary in scientific history, but it is rare to witness one. Until quite recently, we neuroscientists had dismissed more than half of the brain as uninteresting—a humbling realization. We see only now that the glial and neuronal brains work differently, and it is their intimate association that accounts for the astonishing abilities of the brain. Neurons are elegant cells, the brain's information specialists. But the workhorses? Those are the glia.

Referenced

White Matter Matters. R. Douglas Fields in *Scientific American*, Vol. 298, No. 3, pages 54–61; March 2008.

Training Induces Changes in White-Matter Architecture. J. Scholz, M. C. Klein, T.E.J. Behrens and H. Johansen-Berg in *Nature Neuroscience*, Vol. 12, No. 11, pages 1370–1371; November 2009.

Nonsynaptic Communication through ATP Release from Volume-Activated Anion Channels in Axons. R. Douglas Fields and Yingchun Ni in *Science Signaling*, Vol. 3, Issue 142, ra73; October 5, 2010.

Change in the Brain's White Matter. R. Douglas Fields in *Science*, Vol. 330, pages 768–769; November 5, 2010.

Action-Potential Modulation during Axonal Conduction. Takuya Sasaki, Norio Matsuki and Yuji Ikegaya in *Science*, Vol. 331, pages 599-601; February 4, 2011.

The Other Brain. R. Douglas Fields, Simon and Schuster, 2011.

About the Author

R. Douglas Fields is a senior investigator at the National Institutes of Health's Section on Nervous System Development and Plasticity. He is author of Electric Brain: How the New Science of Brainwaves Reads Minds, Tells Us How We Learn, and Helps Us Change for the Better *(BenBella Books, 2020).*

Newfound Hybrid Brain Cells Send Signals like Neurons Do

By Simon Makin

O ur thoughts and feelings arise from networks of neurons, brain cells that send signals using chemicals called neurotransmitters. But neurons aren't alone. They're supported by other cells called glia (Greek for "glue"), which were once thought to hold nerve tissue together. Today glia are known to help regulate metabolism, protect neurons and clean up cellular waste—critical but unglamorous roles.

Now, however, neuroscientists have discovered a type of "hybrid" glia that sends signals using glutamate, the brain's most common neurotransmitter. These findings, published in *Nature*, breach the rigid divide between signaling neurons and supportive glia.

"I hope it's a boost for the field to move forward, to maybe begin studying why certain [brain] circuits have this input and others don't," says study co-author Andrea Volterra, a neuroscientist at the University of Lausanne in Switzerland. Around 30 years ago researchers began reporting that star-shaped glia called astrocytes could communicate with neurons. The idea was controversial, and further research produced contradictory results. To resolve the debate, Volterra and his team analyzed existing data from mouse brains. These data were gathered using a technique called single-cell RNA sequencing, which lets researchers catalog individual cells' molecular profiles instead of averaging them in a bulk tissue sample. Of nine types of astrocytes they found in the hippocampus—a key memory region—one had the cellular machinery required to send glutamate signals.

The small numbers of these cells, present only in certain regions, may explain why earlier research missed them. "It's quite convincing," says neuroscientist Nicola Hamilton-Whitaker of King's College London, who was not involved in the study. "The reason some people may not have seen these specialized functions is they were studying different astrocytes."

Using a technique that visualizes glutamate, the researchers observed the cells in action in live mice. They found that blocking their signaling impaired the mice's memory performance. Further mouse experiments suggested these cells might play a role in epilepsy and Parkinson's disease. Analysis of human RNA databases indicates the same cells may exist in us, but they have not been directly observed.

"People modeling brain circuits never consider these other cells," Hamilton-Whitaker says. "Now we'll all have to agree they're part of the circuit and need to be included to understand how circuits work."

First, neuroscientists must map where in the brain these special cells can be found. Because Volterra's team located them in structures associated with memory, the researchers plan to examine data from people with Alzheimer's disease to see whether, and how, their signaling astrocytes are altered. "We know they're located in memory circuits, so the next question is, What happens in dementia?" Volterra says. "If these cells are modified, they become a new target" for research.

About the Author

Simon Makin is a freelance science journalist based in the U.K. His work has appeared in New Scientist, *the* Economist, Scientific American *and* Nature, *among others. He covers the life sciences and specializes in neuroscience, psychology and mental health. Follow Makin on X (formerly Twitter) @SimonMakin*

Section 2: Memory and Learning

2.1   A Challenge to the Textbooks on How We Learn
       about Our Surroundings
          By Gary Stix

2.2   Emotion Selectively Distorts Our Recollections
          By Ingfei Chen

2.3   Deeper Insights Emerge into How Memories Form
          By R. Douglas Fields

A Challenge to the Textbooks on How We Learn about Our Surroundings

By Gary Stix

D onald Hebb was a famed Canadian scientist who produced key findings that ranged across the field of psychology, providing insights into perception, intelligence and emotion. He is perhaps best known, though, for his theory of learning and memory, which appears as an entry in most basic texts on neuroscience. But now an alternative theory—along with accompanying experimental evidence—fundamentally challenges some central tenets of Hebb's thinking. It provides a detailed account of how cells and the electrical and molecular signals that activate them are involved in forming memories of a series of related events.

Put forward in 1949, Hebb's theory holds that when electrical activity in one neuron—perhaps triggered by observing one's surroundings—repeatedly induces a neighboring "target cell" to fire electrical impulses, a process of conditioning occurs and strengthens the connection between the two neurons. This is a bit like doing arm curls with a weight; after repeated lifts the arm muscle grows stronger and the barbell gets easier to hoist. At the cellular level, repeated stimulation of one neuron by another enables the target cell to respond more readily the next time it is activated. In basic textbooks, this boils down to a simple adage to describe the physiology of learning and memory: "Cells that fire together, wire together."

Every theory requires experimental evidence, and scientists have toiled for years to validate Hebb's idea in the laboratory. Many research findings have showed that when a neuron repeatedly fires off an electrical impulse (called an "action potential") at virtually the same time as an adjacent neuron, their connection does indeed grow more efficient. The target cell fires more easily, and the signal transmitted is stronger. This process—known as long-term potentiation (LTP)—apparently induces physiological change or "plasticity" in target cells.

LTP is routinely cited as a possible explanation for how the brain learns and forms memories at the cellular level.

But long-term potentiation leaves a few open questions. When we encounter something new, the experience often occurs as a sequence of events over at least a matter of seconds—not tiny fractions of a second, as postulated for LTP—and somehow a memory still forms. Nor are many repeated exposures to an event necessarily needed for learning to occur: A child sees the alluring blue and yellow flame on the stove a few feet away. She approaches the stove, slowly raises a finger and then quickly pulls away the hand. Once is enough to learn this lesson for life.

A new paper published in *Science* on September 8 provides evidence for what Jeffrey Magee and other researchers at Howard Hughes Medical Institute's Janelia Research Campus contend is a more plausible explanation for how a sequence of events may form a memory of a place. In their experiments, a mouse running down a track created a memory of a particular spot along the track—a "place field," in neurospeak—over a period of five seconds. The place field was implanted in an area of the brain called the hippocampus after as little as a single traversal of the track.

The action took place in synapses, the tiny clefts between neurons where a signal passes from one cell to another. Visual, tactile or other inputs from another part of the mouse's brain passed through long neuron fibers called axons, crossing over to a target cell in an area called the hippocampus. The inputs trigger the production of a set of signals that persist for several seconds in tiny protrusions, called dendrites, on the hippocampal target cell.

In this form of plasticity, the key signal in the hippocampal cell was not a sub-millisecond action potential, rather it was an electrical signal called a "plateau potential" in the dendrites of the target cell that lasts up to hundreds of times longer. The plateau potential caused a relatively large burst of calcium to enter the target neuron's membrane and this set off a chain of events that lead to molecular and structural changes within the cell itself. After a mouse made just a few runs of the track—sometimes only one—the hippocampal neuron underwent this biochemical learning process and a place field was formed that became active when the mouse passed over the spot again. Thus the animal now "knew" this defined location along the track when the place field activated.

This newly discovered learning process differs in basic ways from the LTP concept long found in textbooks. LTP requires (as Hebb had predicted) that one neuron repeatedly sends an input signal that causes a nearby neuron to fire off submillisecond pulses. Magee and colleagues' discovery—dubbed "behavioral timescale synaptic plasticity"—does not require such a cause-and-effect relationship. One neuron does not induce the firing of another.

Instead, input signals from elsewhere in the brain arrive at the hippocampal neuron several seconds before the calcium spike (the plateau potential) begins in the dendrites. These same input signals persist for several seconds after the plateau potential has ended. The entire five-second time course—the initial inputs followed by a plateau potential and then the inputs that continue afterward—corresponds to the same interval over which a set of actions may occur: the child sees the stove, approaches it, touches the flame and pulls back her hand.

What's more, a new memory of what happened at a particular place is cemented in the brain after a mouse makes one or only a few runs along the track. The researchers also found that when a mouse goes back to the track after this learning process has taken place, a now-trained neuron fires before the animal actually arrives at the spot it has learned—suggesting the memory helps the brain piece out what lies in the physical path ahead.

Magee, the senior author on the study who is now at Baylor College of Medicine, says this new type of plasticity probably will not supplant long-term potentiation in the textbooks. But it may provide a more suitable explanation of how memories are formed from a connected series of events. It may also account for how the brain remembers important places: where a squirrel stores acorns for winter or where a hiker saw a snake on a trail, for instance. "There was always this nagging suspicion that something wasn't quite right about long-term potentiation, and that something was the timing requirement," Magee says. "When you use it to evoke synaptic plasticity, you had to have this really tight timing window. But behavior actually occurs on these much longer timescales—even very simple behaviors." Magee says his group's findings still need to be replicated. And key questions remain, such as where in the brain the signals that serve as inputs to the dendrites originate.

If the work from Magee and his team is further confirmed, LTP may come to be thought of as a process that assists in keeping intact the memories formed by the new type of plasticity discovered by Magee's group—or it may be found to be involved in simpler sensory detection processes that do not require the piecing-together of multiple events. Alcino Silva, a neuroscientist at University of California, Los Angeles, who was not involved with the research, calls the work "a groundbreaking study," and says it "promises to change the way we think about how space is learned and remembered." He adds that the study "is just a provocative beginning." He notes the need for further research to ensure that this finding is "actually key to learning and memory. For example, it will be important to explore this form of plasticity, and then show that manipulating it can both interfere with and enhance specific forms of learning."

Another researcher, György Buzsáki, a neuroscientist at New York University, also not involved in the study, says: "Overall, this is a significant step forward in our understanding of the mechanisms involved in place field generation in the hippocampus." He adds that the neuroscience literature includes examples of various mechanisms for creating such place markers in an animal's brain, including a study his own laboratory that conforms more closely to Hebb's model.

The hippocampus, he says, can also store an internal sequence of events without any sensory inputs of physical surroundings—mental imagery of moving about a place one has never visited, for example—a situation that the behavioral timescale plasticity model discovered by Magee and team may not account for. Whichever model prevails, the new *Science* study provides another example of the constant flux in the brain sciences. A close look at the details of any given process assumed to underlie a long-standing theory can call into question the theory itself, and open up an entirely new avenue of research.

About the Author

Gary Stix, Scientific American's neuroscience and psychology editor, commissions, edits and reports on emerging advances and technologies that have propelled brain science to the forefront of the biological sciences. Developments chronicled in dozens of cover stories, feature articles and news stories, document groundbreaking neuroimaging techniques that reveal what happens in the brain while you are immersed in thought; the arrival of brain implants that alleviate mood disorders like depression; lab-made brains; psychological resilience; meditation; the intricacies of sleep; the new era for psychedelic drugs and artificial intelligence and growing insights leading to an understanding of our conscious selves. Before taking over the neuroscience beat, Stix, as Scientific American's *special projects editor, oversaw the magazine's annual single-topic special issues, conceiving of and producing issues on Einstein, Darwin, climate change, nanotechnology and the nature of time. The issue he edited on time won a National Magazine Award. Besides mind and brain coverage, Stix has edited or written cover stories on Wall Street quants, building the world's tallest building, Olympic training methods, molecular electronics, what makes us human and the things you should and should not eat. Stix started a monthly column, Working Knowledge, that gave the reader a peek at the design and function of common technologies, from polygraph machines to Velcro. It eventually became the magazine's Graphic Science column. He also initiated a column on patents and intellectual property and another on the genesis of the ingenious ideas underlying new technologies in fields like electronics and biotechnology. Stix is the author with his wife, Miriam Lacob, of a technology primer called* Who Gives a Gigabyte: A Survival Guide to the Technologically Perplexed *(John Wiley & Sons, 1999).*

Emotion Selectively Distorts Our Recollections

By Ingfei Chen

O n September 11, 2001, Elizabeth A. Phelps stepped outside her apartment in lower Manhattan and noticed a man staring toward the World Trade Center, about two miles away. Looking up, "I just saw this big, burning hole," Phelps recalls. The man told her that he had just seen a large airplane crash into one of the skyscrapers. Thinking it was a horrible accident, Phelps started walking to work, a few blocks away, for a 9 a.m. telephone meeting. By the time she reached her eighth-floor office at New York University, a second jet had struck the other tower, which collapsed after an hour. Later, she saw the remaining tower fall.

Like Phelps, many Americans have searing memories of that day. In your mind's eye, you can probably relive the moment you first learned of the terrorist attacks: where you were, what you were doing, the shock or fear you experienced. Yet chances are that although they feel real and true, our memories of 9/11 are riddled with errors. "I remember all those details; I'm certain that I'm right," says Phelps, a psychologist. "But the data suggest I'm not."

Recollections of the moment we found out about surprising, traumatic public events are known as flashbulb memories, first described in 1977 by Harvard University psychologists Roger Brown and James Kulik. The idea was that emotionally intense experiences trigger your brain to perfectly record what you are hearing, seeing and feeling—like a camera snapshot when the flash goes off. Stacks of psychology and neuroscience studies indeed show that the human brain is rigged to react to a flood of feelings by activating the key regions that store memories. The brain's recordings, however, are far from flawless reproductions of the original moment.

Research from the past 25 years, including a long-term nationwide survey of 9/11 memories conducted by Phelps and her colleagues, shows that "flashbulb memory" is a misnomer. Memories forged under strong emotions distort considerably even though, paradoxically, they seem so vivid that we hold a misguided confidence in their fidelity.

Although emotion powerfully bolsters our memories of an event, it also edits and sculpts the particulars of what we recall. Such biases or imperfections might seem like a failing of the human brain, but experts note that our emotional memories serve us well most of the time—by preserving the most crucial knowledge for surviving life's challenges. Most people are oblivious to the fact that we possess a heavily edited record of the experiences that move us most. When it comes to remembering, we are more at the mercy of our emotions than we may realize.

Look Here

Amid the endless stream of everyday experience, emotion is like a blazing neon tag that alerts the brain, "Yoo-hoo, this is a moment worth remembering!" The salience of the humdrum sandwich you ate for lunch pales in comparison, consigning its memory to the dustbin. Yet emotions regulate our recall of not just our most riveting moments. Researchers now recognize that the same neural mechanisms involved in flashbulb memories underlie recollections along the continuum of human emotional experience. When people view a series of pictures or words in the laboratory, any emotionally laden content sticks in their head better than neutral information.

Memory is a three-stage process: First comes the learning or encoding of an experience; then, the storage or consolidation of that information over many hours, days and months; and last, the retrieval of that memory when you later relive it. Insights into how emotion modulates this process emerged from studies of conditioned fear responses in rats in the 1980s and 1990s by neuroscientists Joseph E. LeDoux, now at N.Y.U., and James L. McGaugh of the University of California, Irvine, among others. Their work established that the amygdala, a structure buried deep within the brain, orchestrates the memory-boosting effects of fear.

For instance, if you suddenly glimpse a snake while walking in the woods, your amygdala instantly reacts to the snake's threatening features, explains Kevin S. LaBar, a cognitive neuroscientist at Duke University. This region signals your cortex to boost its visual and perceptual processing to confirm that the snake is real, rapidly directing your attention to it. Second, the amygdala triggers the release of stress hormones that set your heart racing and pupils dilating. Those same hormones spur the hippocampus, the memory-encoding center, to start storing or consolidating your perceptions into a neural record. Over the long run, sensory details of the memory are believed to migrate into areas of the cortex for vision, hearing and movement. Later, when you remember that snake, the amygdala and hippocampus are again involved, reigniting the emotional and sensory dimensions of that memory.

The same basic mechanisms also apply for highly arousing, positive events, LaBar explains; activity within the amygdala is associated with many kinds of emotions, not just fear. For instance, in a 2010 study LaBar and his colleagues scanned the brains of diehard college basketball fans and found that the amygdala and hippocampus lit up as the participants remembered exciting plays from a game they watched. In addition, unlike lab studies probing recollections of emotional words or images, the real-world, high-octane basketball memories also engaged social cognition areas involved in recalling situations that include social interactions, LaBar notes. Other studies show that pleasant recollections also activate the brain's reward system. Rather than being limited to a few key brain regions, emotional memory processes are "much more complex than we thought," he says.

Certainly Wrong

Although emotional experiences may initially be etched into memories more strongly than neutral ones, over time they twist away from reality. The first detailed evidence of the inaccurate nature of flashbulb memories emerged from surveys done after the space shuttle *Challenger* exploded in 1986. The recent analyses of 9/11 memories have further clarified what is and is not special about these intense remembrances. On September 12, 2001, Duke psychologists Jennifer M. Talarico and David C. Rubin surveyed students' memories of 9/11 and a more prosaic but notable event from the preceding weekend, such as a birthday party or study group session. In retests during the following year, accuracy of details declined equally in both types of memory. The clarity and confidence they reported in their recollections varied: the students consistently rated their memory of 9/11 as being much more vivid than it was for the ordinary occurrences.

"They thought it was much more accurate," says Talarico, now at Lafayette College. In other words, she says, what distinguishes flashbulb memories is "this sense of enhanced vividness and inflated confidence that we have in the accuracy, this sense that I will never forget 'X.'"

A similar pattern was seen in the nationwide 9/11 memory project. Phelps and psychologist William Hirst of the New School for Social Research and their colleagues surveyed more than 3,000 volunteers in New York City, Washington, D.C., and five other cities one week after the attacks, in subsequent years and again this past summer. (Ten-year data are still being analyzed.) Compared with their initial reports, Hirst says, participants were only 63 percent correct on the when-where-how types of details about learning of the attack one year after 9/11; after that, the decline slowed. Yet they were "absolutely confident that their memory was correct," he says.

Surprisingly, people were worst at describing their emotional state on 9/11, with only 42 percent of them right a year later. Initial shock may give way to sadness or frustration with time, Hirst explains, and we tend to "reconstruct our emotional past in a way that's consistent with the way we currently are emotionally reacting."

Survey takers showed better accuracy for the central facts of the terrorist event, such as the number of hijacked planes and crash sites. "Societal memory practices" such as watching media coverage and talking about 9/11 with others had a major influence.

"Our memory is just not independent of the larger social context in which we exist," Hirst says.

Emotional Tunnel Vision

Our gut reactions to the world affect the brain's cataloguing efforts in several distinct ways. For one thing, emotion is selective in how it enhances memory. Experts noticed long ago the "weapon focus effect"—a witness might confidently testify to seeing the gun held by a robber and yet recall little of his face. Many other lab studies have observed the same kind of tunnel vision: individuals remember a picture of a snake in a forest better than a scene of a chipmunk set in a similar background. Although people vividly recall the snake, they tend to forget the surrounding forest, says cognitive neuroscientist Elizabeth A. Kensinger of Boston College. "Their memory for that emotional item"—the snake—"actually seems to be coming at the cost of their memory for the context."

That trade-off can partly be explained by the way an emotionally arousing object grabs your attention. Countless stimuli vie for your notice, says psychologist Mara Mather of the University of Southern California. What wins out might be something eye-catching or startling, such as a bright object flitting across the grass, or it might be something you are deliberately trying to focus on, such as a phone call, while consciously screening out distractions.

Emotions magnify this effect, intensifying the attention-snagging property of a stimulus, Mather believes. Thus, whatever dominates your mind ends up in the memory banks. That idea may help explain why, in seemingly contradictory studies, scientists have observed participants showing stronger memory for neutral details in an emotional scene. Say you are walking past a man, and a gunshot suddenly rings out from up the street. Under Mather's theory, someone who was nondescript to begin with would be even less memorable after the gunshot. Yet if you had already looked at the gentleman closely because he resembled a friend, "you would actually remember that face even better if there were a gunshot afterward," she says. The emotional nature of the situation would burn this bystander into your mind, as a kind of side effect, even though he had nothing to do with the real action.

Some research suggests that positive, highly arousing events, such as a marriage proposal or winning a prize, trigger a similar trade-off, Kensinger says. Uplifting memories, on the other hand, may differ in the type of information that is preserved, she notes, based on functional MRI studies she and her colleagues published in 2008. Whereas the scary snake-in-the-forest scenario fires up the brain's sensory processing regions, perhaps leading to a crystal-clear memory of the snake's stripes, positive excitement may instead stimulate areas in the frontal lobe that process concepts, Kensinger points out. It may, for example, train your memory toward happy thoughts about how you might spend a wad of cash that was just handed to you, rather than on what the cash looked like. "It seems like a lot of those perceptual details just are not retained with the same resolution for positive information as they are for negative information," Kensinger says. Happy memories also appear prone to distortions in accuracy and confidence—in some studies, even more so than negative recollections.

What you remember about an emotional event may also depend on your personality and age. In a 2010 study Kensinger and her colleagues found that people who reported higher everyday anxiety were more likely to exhibit the emotional memory trade-off—better retention of the main emotional features but a weaker grasp of the neutral background information—than those with less anxiety. The memories of older adults are biased in a different way; they swing toward being more positive. Mather and her associates observed in a 2003 study that after viewing a series of images ranging from, say, a cockroach on a pizza slice to the face of a smiling baby, older adults favored the happy images: half of the images the elders correctly recalled were positive and slightly more than a quarter were negative (the rest were neutral), compared with 36 percent positive, 40 percent negative for the younger participants. The effect does not seem to arise from any age-related decline in the amygdala's radar for threatening signals, Mather says. Instead older adults appear to actively manage their emotions by paying less attention to negative things.

Sleep on It

After an emotional event, increasing evidence shows, another factor has a potent hand in pruning and transforming the brain's recollection of it: sleep. "The sleeping brain seems to somehow make calculations about what to remember and what to forget," says cognitive neuroscientist Jessica D. Payne of the University of Notre Dame.

How sleep meddles with memories, however, is complex. In one study, Payne, Kensinger and their colleagues asked volunteers to look closely at chipmunk- or snake-in-the-forest types of scenes and then tested whether they recognized various components of those images after 30 minutes and again 12 hours later. One group did the experiment during the daytime, and a second group got a night of sleep before the final memory test. As expected, everyone showed enhanced memory for the emotional scenes over the neutral ones, as well as better recall for the snake but not the surrounding forest. This selectivity was even more pronounced after sleep, Payne says: whereas the memories of the entire snake scene showed some deterioration after 12 hours in those who stayed awake, the sleepers actually had better recollection of the snake and worse retention of the forest. Yet slumber offered no memory benefit for the nonemotional chipmunk scene. As Payne explains, sleep "selectively preserves only the emotional aspect of the scene."

At the University of California, Berkeley, neuroscientist Matthew P. Walker is exploring an intriguing new hypothesis that sleep also helps to soothe the sharp edges of bad memories. In particular, Walker notes that numerous studies have shown that during rapid eye movement, or "dream" sleep, the hippocampus and amygdala reactivate, yet some arousal-inducing stress hormones, particularly noradrenaline, are suppressed. The lack of those stress hormones may let the brain process emotional memories in what seems like a safe environment. During slumber, he theorizes, the brain strengthens its memory of the information within a distressing episode while "stripping away the emotional tone."

If that mechanism fails, the result could be chronic anxiety or the recurring nightmares of post-traumatic stress disorder, Walker says. Experiments by his lab also suggest that the chronic lack of sound sleep that is common in those disorders and in depression may even skew memories toward gloom, possibly perpetuating symptoms.

Good Enough?

What should we make of the fact that our most cherished memories may not be entirely true? Experts are quick to answer that these recollections typically do bear a hardy kernel of truth. "Our memory is good enough to get through the day," Hirst says, noting that accuracy concerns did not come up in humanity's ancient past, when neither tape recorders nor written accounts could serve as references. Yet human memory may not be sufficiently solid to offer reliable eyewitness testimony in courts, he says. There the devil may be in the details, such as whether an alleged bank robber drove off in a Honda or a Toyota SUV, and those details of a heated moment are especially fluid in memory. The challenge for psychologists, Phelps says, is to clearly define where and when people's memories of emotionally fraught incidents tend to break down. To that end, her group has unpublished results suggesting that people have more accurate recall for the place and the timing of an emotional event than for other aspects, such as who first told them about it.

An even greater mystery is why emotion infuses our memories with such a supreme yet misplaced confidence. "You can't even convince people that their memories are wrong," Phelps says. Usually when you feel certain about many facets of a run-of-the-mill recollection, you are right. With emotional events, however, your vivid memory for a few central, correct facts seems to foster the mistaken impression that it is good for all details, Phelps says.

Why this disconnect? Enhanced confidence lets you react more quickly during a similar crisis in the future, Phelps theorizes. People do not forget the gist of 9/11, and if you saw a plane flying near a skyscraper you were in, she notes, "you would get out, right now."

Experts believe that human memory evolved not to provide a static, high-fidelity record of the past but to help us prepare for an unpredictable future. A malleable memory lends a powerful advantage: "You can add and change things as you need to," Payne says. That flexibility allows our brain to restructure what we have learned, make generalizations across concepts and experiences, and brainstorm new ideas.

Remaking Memories

At times, though, you might prefer an accurate account over the benefits of fluid learning. By realizing that memory naturally zooms in on the most emotionally evocative aspects of an experience, you may be able to broaden your attention to override that bias. "You can make some effort to actually now focus on the nonemotional things that might be important," Phelps says. Police officers are trained in such tactics for assessing crime scenes, she notes: faced with a dead body in a motel room, homicide detectives would not only examine the corpse but also control their emotional responses to it and carefully scan around the bed or bathroom for possible clues.

Another potential way to enhance accuracy in emotional memories while also damping down their negative overtones is to put a positive spin on a bad situation—a technique called cognitive reappraisal. In a study published in 2010 LaBar, Jasmeet Pannu Hayes, a psychologist now at Boston University , and their colleagues asked people—while they were in a brain scanner—to either suppress their emotional reactions as they viewed distressing scenes or appraise them more favorably. If shown an injured man in a hospital bed, the participants could imagine that excellent care would help him heal. Compared with the suppressors, the reappraisers reported less emotional distress on seeing the unpleasant pictures and showed better memory for the images two weeks later. In the reappraisers, the hippocampus got "a double whammy" of stimulation, LaBar says: One boost came from the amygdala reacting to the negative scenes even though its response had been muted by the reappraisal process. A second communiqué came from the left inferior prefrontal cortex, which helps to process information deeply and showed greater activity in the reappraisal group. (In the suppression group, the hippocampus communicated less with these other brain regions, resulting in poorer memory for the scenes.)

By using the strategy of positive thinking in a stressful circumstance, "you've lowered the emotional arousal, but you still have a good memory of it," LaBar says. Reappraisal is the basis of cognitive-behavior treatment for various psychological disorders.

The possibilities for refining our emotional memories are intriguing. Yet with the passage of time, human memory is inevitably a fragile, fading thing. Societies compensate for this frailty by holding anniversaries and memorials that revive the memory of loved ones lost—and by inventing gizmos such as tape recorders and cell-phone cameras that help us never forget.

Referenced

Beyond Fear: Emotional Memory Mechanisms in the Human Brain. Kevin S. LaBar in *Current Directions in Psychological Science*, Vol. 16, No. 4, pages 173–177; 2007.

How (and Why) Emotion Enhances the Subjective Sense of Recollection. Elizabeth A. Phelps and Tali Sharot in *Current Directions in Psychological Science*, Vol. 17, No. 2, pages 147–152; 2008.

Long-Term Memory for the Terrorist Attack of September 11: Flashbulb Memories, Event Memories, and the Factors That Influence Their Retention. William Hirst et al. in *Journal of Experimental Psychology: General*, Vol. 138, No. 2, pages 161–176; 2009.

Remembering the Details: Effects of Emotion. Elizabeth A. Kensinger in *Emotion Review*, Vol. 1, No. 2, pages 99–113; 2009.

Sleep and Emotional Memory Processing. Els van der Helm and Matthew P. Walker in *Sleep Medicine Clinics*, Vol. 6, No. 1, pages 31–43; March 2011.

Forgetting about 9/11. Ingrid Wickelgren in *Streams of Consciousness* blog: http://blogs.scientificamerican.com/streams-of-consciousness/2011/09/01/forgetting-about-911

How Accurate Are Memories of 9/11? Ingfei Chen in Ask the Experts, *Scientific American* online, September 6, 2011. www.scientificamerican.com/article.cfm?id=911-memory-accuracy

Deeper Insights Emerge into How Memories Form

By R. Douglas Fields

Neuroscientists have always presumed that learning and memory depend on strengthening or weakening the connection points between neurons (synapses), increasing or decreasing the likelihood that the cell is going to pass along a message to its neighbor. But recently some researchers have started pursuing a completely different theory that does not involve changing the strength of synaptic transmission; in fact, it does not even involve neurons. Instead other types of brain cells, called glia, are responsible.

A new study from the University of Toronto, published online this week in the journal *Neuron*, furnishes support for this theory. It provides evidence that the basic act of learning whether one's environs are safe or not, a behavior common to all animals, depends on glial cells that form the fatty sheath called myelin—electrical insulation that covers nerve fibers. The new theory postulates that establishing indelible memories that can be recalled long after sensory input or training on a task involves an interaction between glia and peculiar brain waves produced during sleep. "The role of myelin in cognitive functions has been largely neglected, an omission elegantly rectified by this paper," says myelin researcher Bernard Zalc, at the Sorbonne Université in Paris, commenting on this new study.

Traditionally researchers who study the myelin insulation on nerve fibers, called axons, have focused on diseases, such as multiple sclerosis, in which the fatty sheath is damaged. In multiple sclerosis, neural transmission fails, causing wide-ranging disabilities. Much like the plastic coating on a copper wire, myelin was understood to be vital for neural transmission but inert and irrelevant to information processing and memory storage.

The new research challenges that view because of the discovery that the glial cells that form myelin, called oligodendrocytes, can detect neural impulses flowing thorough the axons they contact. Intriguingly, immature oligodendrocytes, called oligodendrocyte progenitor cells (OPCs), populate nearly the entire brain with little regard for the complex anatomical boundaries within brain tissue. Salted throughout the brain—even in adulthood when there would seem to be little need for immature brain cells—OPCs are by far the most abundant cells undergoing cell division in our brain.

Why that is, is unclear, and these peculiar cells have long mystified researchers. Research in several laboratories has found recently that OPCs can respond to neural impulse activity by dividing and maturing into myelin-forming oligodendrocytes, and increasing the number of myelinated axons. This process could have a profound effect on information transfer through neural networks because myelin boosts the speed of neural impulse transmission by about 50 times.

Forming Memories

In the *Neuron* study, first author Patrick Steadman and colleagues in the laboratory of Paul Frankland at the Hospital for Sick Children and University of Toronto, tested the hypothesis that new myelin must form during learning. They did so by genetically altering mice so that a gene called myelin regulatory factor (MRF) is deleted when treated with the drug tamoxifen. The gene is essential for OPCs to mature into oligodendrocytes. Knocking out MRF increased the number of OPCs, whereas the number of newly formed oligodendrocytes diminished.

Now the researchers could test the hypothesis that formation of myelin is necessary for learning by training these mice while preventing them from forming new myelin. They could block myelin formation at any point during training or afterward simply by administering tamoxifen to the mice.

They then probed whether myelin is needed for learning by giving a well-established memory test called the Morris water maze, in which a mouse is placed in a large tub of water in which a hidden platform is submerged just below the surface. The mice quickly learned where

45

that platform was, and they swam directly to it after several days of training. The experiments showed that the mice that were unable to form new myelin were able to learn where the platform was just as quickly as control mice, but when their recall was tested long after training ended, the ones that could not form new myelin did not remember the location as well and had to swim for a longer time to find the platform again. Examining the brain tissue with an electron microscope, the researchers found that more axons were myelinated in regions of the brains of normal mice known to be required for learning the Morris water maze. The researchers now had evidence that myelin is involved in making the long-term memories involved in learning. But they still needed to pin down myelin's role in recall.

Arriving on Time

Different types of information must be brought together at the same time to recall, for example, where your home is located—or, for a mouse, the platform in the water maze. Recall requires the integration of memories of sights, sounds, smells, emotions related to your home, and sensations the memory of your home evokes. These diverse types of information are processed and stored in very different parts of the brain and connected by broad-ranging networks that must be activated together to interlace diverse aspects of these memories, ultimately resulting, at the subcellular level, in the strengthening of synapses. This network-centric view of neural functioning has been overlooked by memory researchers narrowly focused on synaptic transmission. But the question still remains of how the arrival time of neural impulses at each synaptic relay point in complex neural networks is established. The brain rhythms of sleep may provide a clue.

The researchers wondered if new myelin might be necessary after the training was over to convert a short-term memory that quickly fades away into a long-lasting memory, a process neuroscientists call memory consolidation. To test that idea, they trained the mice, as before, three times a day for six days and then administered tamoxifen after the training had ended to inhibit myelin formation.

When tested 28 days later, the mice that could not form new myelin after the training session performed poorly in recalling where the hidden platform was. If they waited too long after training to inhibit the formation of new myelin—25 days in their tests—recall was not impaired, indicating that a window of time persists after training when new experiences become consolidated into memory. The results suggest that new myelin is part of the process of engraving lasting memories. But the researchers drilled down still further to ask how specifically does myelin promote memory consolidation? To answer that, the researchers turned their investigation to a different learning situation that induced fearful memories in the animals.

Making Memories During Sleep

A soldier riding in a jeep in Afghanistan will feel an intense sensation of danger from the risk of a roadside bomb, but will relax riding in a jeep through the streets of his hometown. The hippocampus is the brain's "GPS" system that determines the location of the body in the environment, but higher-level cognitive functions processed in the prefrontal cortex are necessary to provide the context of whether a location is associated with a friend or a foe. When communication between the hippocampus and prefrontal cortex becomes impaired after a traumatic experience, the body's fear response can be activated inappropriately, causing a person with PTSD to suffer the same intense sense of danger while riding in a jeep at home. Because this type of memory requires long-distance communication between brain regions, it could provide insight into how myelin consolidates memory.

Scientists study this type of fearful learning by placing an experimental animal in a cage where a harmless but alarming electric shock is applied through the metal floor after a warning sound. The animal will freeze in fear later when the same alarm sound is presented in the same cage, even without the foot shock. However, the animal will not freeze in response to the same sound in a different environment, because it is not associated with the induced fear. The communication between the hippocampus and prefrontal cortex provides the essential context that sparks the varying reactions. Research by György Buzsáki at New York University discovered that brief, high-frequency oscillations in the hippocampus—brain waves called sharp wave/ripple complexes—convey information by coupling in synchrony with cortical neurons firing rhythmically in what are called spindle oscillations. Promoting this rhythmic coupling can improve memory consolidation.

These unusual waves of rhythmic neural activity are especially active during non-REM (dreamless) sleep, and learning a new task increases this activity. It is believed that this transfer of information between the hippocampus and prefrontal cortex during sleep links the memory of place with its context. In my own research, we have found that myelin is important for transmission of brain waves, raising the possibility that the need for new myelin in memory consolidation could promote this shuttling of information between hippocampus and prefrontal cortex by these unusual neural oscillations.

Brain waves oscillate at many different frequencies. Two regions of the brain oscillating together in synchrony may promote the coupling of distant populations of neurons into functional assemblies. Much like the synchronization of the string section and French horns in an orchestra, synchronous brain rhythms could potentially couple neurons in the prefrontal cortex and hippocampus together for the mouse to learn to fear a particular location. Myelin could play a key role in regulating the speed of transmission of brain waves. If waves of neural activity are not transmitted at the proper rate, destructive interference of one wave with another will disrupt the transmission of rhythmic information in the brain—just as musicians playing out of time will mangle a symphonic work.

Interestingly, changes in myelin have been found during sleep and sleep deprivation. Steadman and colleagues tested whether the formation of myelin during sleep may promote learning by increasing the coupling of brain wave activity by recording neural oscillations in the hippocampus and prefrontal cortex of mice. They found that when the formation of new myelin was impaired by deleting the MRF gene, the synchrony of brain wave coupling was indeed reduced and the animals performed poorly in invoking the memory of fear learned in the environment where they had been shocked. .

Together these studies indicate that formation of new myelin is necessary for learning because it consolidates memories by facilitating the coordinated brain wave activity between the hippocampus and prefrontal cortex. New myelin also appears to be needed for other types of learning—in improving motor coordination, for example. "When we think about how memories are consolidated, traditionally we have always thought about synaptic plasticity. Our findings suggest that an entirely distinct form of plasticity [myelin plasticity] also plays a critical role in consolidating memories," Frankland says. One well-known researcher on how memories are made, James McGaugh of the University of California, Irvine, agrees: "The paper reports novel and very highly interesting findings that ... suggest new directions for understanding how memories are formed."

Minding the strengthening and weakening of synapses is critical for learning, but so is getting to the station on time to make the right connections, and that's where nonneuronal cells making myelin to speed transmission through neural networks assist in forming new memories.

About the Author

R. Douglas Fields is a senior investigator at the National Institutes of Health's Section on Nervous System Development and Plasticity. He is author of Electric Brain: How the New Science of Brainwaves Reads Minds, Tells Us How We Learn, and Helps Us Change for the Better *(BenBella Books, 2020).*

Section 3: Techniques in Brain Research

3.1 Controlling the Brain with Light
By Karl Deisseroth

3.2 A Cell Atlas Reveals the Biodiversity inside Our Head
By Christof Koch, Hongkui Zeng, and Ed S. Lein

3.3 "Mini Brains" Are Not like the Real Thing
By Karen Weintraub

3.4 The Fading Dream of the Computer Brain
By Noah Hutton

Controlling the Brain with Light

By Karl Deisseroth

Every day as a practicing psychiatrist, I confront my field's limitations. Despite the noble efforts of clinicians and researchers, our limited insight into the roots of psychiatric disease hinders the search for cures and contributes to the stigmatization of this enormous problem, the leading cause worldwide of years lost to death or disability. Clearly, we need new answers in psychiatry. But as philosopher of science Karl Popper might have said, before we can find the answers, we need the power to ask new questions. In other words, we need new technology.

Developing appropriate techniques is difficult, however, because the mammalian brain is beyond compare in its complexity. It is an intricate system in which tens of billions of intertwined neurons—with multitudinous distinct characteristics and wiring patterns—exchange precisely timed, millisecond-scale electrical signals and a rich diversity of biochemical messengers. Because of that complexity, neuroscientists lack a deep grasp of what the brain is really doing—of how specific activity patterns within specific brain cells ultimately give rise to thoughts, memories, sensations and feelings. By extension, we also do not know how the brain's physical failures produce distinct psychiatric disorders such as depression or schizophrenia. The ruling paradigm of psychiatric disorders—casting them in terms of chemical imbalances and altered levels of neurotransmitters—does not do justice to the brain's high-speed electrical neural circuitry. Psychiatric treatments are thus essentially serendipitous: helpful for many but rarely illuminating.

Little wonder, then, that in a 1979 *Scientific American* article, Nobel laureate Francis Crick suggested that the major challenge facing neuroscience was the need to control one type of cell in the brain while leaving others unaltered. Electrical stimuli cannot meet this challenge, because electrodes are too crude a tool: they stimulate all the cells at their insertion site without distinguishing between different cell types, and their signals also cannot turn neurons off with precision. Crick later speculated in lectures that light could serve as a control tool because it could be delivered in precisely timed pulses in a range of colors and locations, but at the time no one had any idea about how specific cells could be made to respond to light.

Meanwhile, in a realm of biology as distant from the study of the mammalian brain as might seem possible, researchers were working on microorganisms that would only much later turn out to be relevant. At least 40 years ago biologists knew that some microorganisms produce proteins that directly regulate the flow of electric charge across their membranes in response to visible light. These proteins, which are produced by a characteristic set of "opsin" genes, help to extract energy and information from the light in the microbes' environments. In 1971 Walther Stoeckenius and Dieter Oesterhelt, both then at the University of California, San Francisco, discovered that one of these proteins, bacteriorhodopsin, acts as a single-component ion pump that can be briefly activated by photons of green light—a remarkable all-in-one molecular machine. Later identification of other members of this family of proteins—the halorhodopsins in 1977 and the channelrhodopsins in 2002—continued this original theme from 1971 of single-gene, all-in-one control.

In 20/20 hindsight, the solution to Crick's challenge—a strategy to dramatically advance brain research—was therefore available in principle even before he articulated it. Yet it took more than 30 years for the concepts to come together in the new technology of optogenetics.

Optogenetics is the combination of genetics and optics to control well-defined events within any specific cells of living tissue (not just those of the nervous system). It includes the discovery and insertion into cells of genes that confer light responsiveness; it also includes the associated technologies for delivering light into the brain, directing the light's effect to genes and cells of interest, and assessing readouts, or effects of this optical control. What excites neuroscientists about optogenetics is that it provides control over defined events within defined cell types at defined times—a level of precision that is not only fundamentally new but most likely crucial to biological understanding.

The significance of any event in a cell is understandable only in the context of the other events occurring around it in the rest of the tissue, the whole organism or even the larger environment. Even a shift of a few milliseconds in the timing of a neuron's firing, for example, can sometimes completely reverse the effect of its signal on the rest of the nervous system. Thousands of scientists are now wielding optogenetics to learn how specific activity patterns within select sets of neurons lead to complex physiology and behavior in worms, flies, fish, birds, mice, rats and monkeys. The work has already yielded important insights into human problems, including depression, disordered sleep, Parkinson's disease and schizophrenia.

Casting Light on Life

Biology has a tradition of using light to intervene in living systems. Researchers have long employed a light-based method called CALI to destroy, and thus inhibit, selected proteins; lasers have also been used to destroy specific cells, for example, in the worm *Caenorhabditis elegans*. Conversely, Richard L. Fork of Bell Laboratories (in the 1970s) and Rafael Yuste of Columbia University (in 2002) reported ways to stimulate neurons with lasers that partially disrupted cell membranes. In the past decade the laboratories of Gero Miesenböck, while at Memorial Sloan-Kettering Cancer Center, and of Ehud Isacoff, Richard H. Kramer and Dirk Trauner, then all at the University of California, Berkeley, have employed multicomponent systems for modulating targeted cells with light. They introduced, for example, both a protein that regulates neurons and a chemical that would spur the protein into action when triggered by ultraviolet light.

Yet destroying proteins or cells of interest obviously limits one's experimental options, and methods that depend on multiple components, though elegant and useful, entail practical challenges and have not had broad applicability or utility in mammals. A fundamental shift to a single-component strategy was necessary. As it turned out, this single-component strategy was not able to build on any of the parts or methods from earlier approaches but instead employed the remarkable all-in-one light-activated proteins from microbes: bacteriorhodopsins, halorhodopsins and channelrhodopsins.

In 2000, well after bacteriorhodopsin and halorhodopsin had become known to science, the Kazusa DNA Research Institute in Japan posted online thousands of new gene sequences from the green algae *Chlamydomonas reinhardtii*. While reviewing them, Peter Hegemann, then at Regensburg University in Berlin, who had predicted that *Chlamydomonas* would have a light-activated ion channel, noticed two long sequences similar to those for bacteriorhodopsin, obtained copies of them from Kazusa and asked Georg Nagel (then a principal investigator in Frankfurt) to test if they indeed coded for ion channels. In 2002 Hegemann and Nagel described their finding that one of these sequences encoded a single-protein membrane channel responsive to blue light: when hit by blue photons, it regulated the flow of positively charged ions. The protein was consequently dubbed channelrhodopsin-1, or ChR1. The following year Nagel and Hegemann (along with their colleagues, including Ernst Bamberg in Frankfurt) explored the other sequence and named the encoded protein channelrhodopsin-2, or ChR2. Almost simultaneously, John L. Spudich of University of Texas Medical School at Houston separately provided evidence that those genes were important to the light-dependent responses of *Chlamydomonas*. Yet the discovery of these channelrhodopsins—a third type of single-component light-activated ion-conductance protein—did not immediately translate into an advance in neuroscience any more than the discoveries of bacteriorhodopsins and halorhodopsins in previous decades had.

A number of scientists have confided to me that they had considered inserting bacterial or algal opsin genes in neurons and trying to control the altered cells with light but had abandoned the idea. Animal cells were unlikely to manufacture the microbial proteins efficiently or safely, and the proteins were virtually certain to be too slow and weak to be effective. Furthermore, to function, the proteins would require an additional cofactor—a vitamin A–related compound called all-trans retinal to absorb the photons. The risk of wasting time and money was far too great.

Nevertheless, for the bioengineering research team I had assembled at Stanford University, the motivation to improve understanding in clinical psychiatry was more than enough to justify the extremely high risk of failure. During my psychiatric residency, I had witnessed firsthand the weaknesses and side effects of medications and treatments such as electroconvulsive therapy. This experience contributed to my willingness to take the plunge, and so as a principal investigator at Stanford in 2004 I formed a team that included graduate students Edward S. Boyden and Feng Zhang to address this challenge. I introduced channelrhodopsin-2 into mammalian neurons in culture by the well-established techniques of transfection—that is, by splicing the gene for ChR2 and a specific kind of on switch, or promoter, into the genes of a vector (such as a benign virus) that ferried the added genetic material into the cells. Promoters can ensure that only selected kinds of neurons (such as only those able to secrete the neurotransmitter glutamate) will express, or make, the encoded opsin proteins.

Against all odds, the experiment worked—and worked surprisingly well. Using nothing more than safe pulses of visible light, we attained reliable, millisecond-precision control over the cells' patterns of firing of action potentials—the voltage blips, or impulses, that enable one neuron to convey information to another. In August 2005 my team published the first report that by introducing a single microbial opsin gene into mammalian neurons, we could make the cells precisely responsive to light. Channelrhodopsins (and, eventually as we found, the bacteriorhodopsin from 1971 and the halorhodopsins, too) all proved able to turn neurons on or off, efficiently and safely in response to light. They worked in part because, in an unexpected gift from nature, mammalian tissues happen to contain naturally robust quantities of all-trans retinal—the one chemical cofactor essential for photons to activate microbial opsins—so nothing beyond an opsin gene needs to be added to targeted neurons.

Our initial report appeared in 2005, and a year later my Stanford colleague Mark Schnitzer and I named the approach "optogenetics" in a review paper. By then, laboratories across the world were employing it, using versions of these genes that my team had synthesized to work optimally in mammalian cells. As of today, we have sent those genes to around 700 labs.

Improving on Nature

The number of optogenetic tools, along with the variety of their capabilities, has expanded rapidly because of an astonishing convergence of ecology and engineering. Investigators are adding new opsins to their tool kit by scouring the natural world for novel ones; they are also applying molecular engineering to tweak the known opsins to make them even more useful for diverse experiments in a wider range of organisms.

In 2008, for instance, our genome searches led by Feng Zhang on a different algal species, *Volvox carteri*, revealed a third channelrhodopsin (VChR1), which responds to yellow light instead of blue, as we showed with Hegemann. Using VChR1 and the other channelrhodopsins together, we can simultaneously control mixed populations of cells, with yellow light exerting one type of control over some of them and blue light sending a different command to others. And we now have found that the most potent channelrhodopsin of all is actually a hybrid of VChR1 and ChR1 (with no contribution at all from ChR2). Our other modified opsins (created with Ofer Yizhar, Lief Fenno, Lisa Gunaydin, and Hegemann and his students) now include "ultrafast" and "ultraslow" channelrhodopsin mutants that offer exquisite control over the timing and duration of action potentials: the former can drive action potentials more than 200 times per second, whereas the latter can push cells into or out of stable excitable states with single pulses of light. Our newest opsins can also now respond to deep red light bordering on the infrared, which stays more sharply focused, penetrates tissues more easily and is very well tolerated.

Molecular engineering has also extended optogenetic control beyond cells' electrical behaviors to their biochemistry. A large fraction of all approved medical drugs act on a family of membrane proteins called G-protein-coupled receptors. These proteins sense extracellular signaling chemicals, such as epinephrine, and respond by changing the levels of intracellular biochemical signals, such as calcium ions, and thus the activity of the cells. By adding the light-sensing domain from a rhodopsin molecule to G-protein-coupled receptors, Raag D. Airan and others in my laboratory developed a set of receptors called optoXRs that respond rapidly to green light. When viruses insert genetic constructs for optoXRs into the brains of lab rodents, the optoXRs provide us with control over biochemical events in the animals while they are moving freely within a cage. Fast and cell type–specific optical control over biochemical pathways is now therefore possible, both in laboratory dishes and in untethered mammals; this control over biochemistry opens the door to optogenetics in essentially every cell and tissue in biology.

Many of the natural opsin genes now being discovered in various microbes' genomes encode proteins that mammalian cells do not make well. But Viviana Gradinaru in my group has developed a number of general-purpose strategies for improving their delivery and expression. For example, pieces of DNA can be bundled with the opsin genes to act as "zip codes" to ensure the genes are transported to the correct compartments within mammalian cells and translated properly into functional proteins. And with fiber-optic tools we developed in 2006 and 2007, investigators can now deliver light for optogenetic control to any area of the brain—whether surface or deep—in freely moving mammals. And to enable simultaneous readouts of the dynamic electrical signals elicited by optogenetic control, we have developed millisecond-scale instruments that are integrated hybrids of fiber optics and electrodes (which we call "optrodes").

A beautiful synergy can emerge between optical stimulation and electrical recording because the two can be set up to not interfere with each other. We can now, for instance, directly observe the changing electrical activity in the neural circuits involved in motor control at the same time as we are optically controlling those circuits with microbial opsins. The more rich and complex the optogenetic inputs and electrical outputs of neural circuits become, the more we will be able to move toward a form of reverse engineering for neural circuitry: we will be able to infer the computational and informational roles of neural circuits from how they transform our signals. Reverse-engineering healthy neural circuits will offer wonderful opportunities for determining which properties and activities differ in psychiatric and neurological disease states. That knowledge, in turn, should help guide efforts to find interventions able to restore normalcy in those circuits.

Reverse-Engineering the Mind

The importance of optogenetics as a research tool, particularly in conjunction with other technologies, continues to grow rapidly. In recent years neuroscience has made many advances based on the brain-scanning technique called functional magnetic resonance imaging (fMRI). These scans are usually billed as providing detailed maps of neural activity in response to various stimuli. Yet strictly speaking, fMRI only shows changes in blood-oxygen levels in different areas of the brain, and those changes are just a proxy for actual neural activity.

Some nagging uncertainty has therefore always surrounded the question of whether these complex signals can be triggered by increases in local excitatory neural activity. This past May, however, my laboratory used a combination of optogenetics and fMRI (ofMRI) to verify that the firing of local excitatory neurons is fully sufficient to trigger the complex signals detected by fMRI scanners. In addition, the pairing of optogenetics and fMRI can map functional neural circuits with an exactness and completeness not previously possible with electrodes or drugs. Optogenetics is thereby helping to validate and advance a wealth of scientific literature in neuroscience and psychiatry.

Indeed, the impact of optogenetics has already been felt directly on some questions of human disease. In animals, we have employed optogenetics on a kind of neuron (hypocretin cells) deep in a part of the brain previously implicated in the sleep disorder narcolepsy. Specific types of electrical activity in those neurons, we have found, set off awakening. Finding a way to induce that neural activity clinically might therefore offer a treatment someday, but most important is the scientific insight that specific kinds of activity in specific cells can produce complex behaviors.

Optogenetics is also helping to determine how dopamine-making neurons may give rise to feelings of reward and pleasure. My team optogenetically induced differently timed bursts of activity in well-defined sets of dopamine neurons in freely moving mice. We identified the stimulus patterns that appeared to drive a sense of reward for the animals. In the absence of any other cue or reward, mice chose to spend more time in places where they had received particular kinds of bursts of activity in their dopamine neurons. This information is useful for teasing out the cellular activity underlying both the normal reward process and the pleasure-system pathologies involved in depression and substance abuse.

The optogenetic approach has also improved our understanding of Parkinson's, which involves a disturbance of information processing in certain motor-control circuits of the brain. Since the 1990s some Parkinson's patients have received a measure of relief from a therapy called deep-brain stimulation, in which an implanted device similar to a pacemaker applies carefully timed oscillating electric stimuli to certain areas far inside the brain, such as the subthalamic nucleus.

Yet the promise of this technique for Parkinson's (and indeed for a variety of other conditions) is partially limited because electrodes stimulate nearby brain cells unselectively and medical understanding of what stimuli to apply is woefully incomplete. Recently, however, we have used optogenetics to study animal models of Parkinson's and gained fundamental insight into the nature of the diseased circuitry and the mechanisms of action of therapeutic interventions.

We have found, for example, that deep-brain stimulation may be most effective when it targets not cells but rather the connections between cells—affecting the flow of activity between brain regions.

And with our colleague Anatol Kreitzer of U.C.S.F., we functionally mapped two pathways in brain movement circuitry: one that slows movements and one that speeds them up and can counteract the parkinsonian state.

We have also learned how to prod one kind of cell, neocortical parvalbumin neurons, to modulate 40-cycles-per-second rhythms in brain activity called gamma oscillations. Science has known for some time that schizophrenic patients have altered parvalbumin cells and that gamma oscillations are abnormal in both schizophrenia and autism—but the causal meaning of these correlations (if any) was not known. Using optogenetics, we showed that parvalbumin cells serve to enhance gamma waves and that those waves in turn enhance the flow of information through cortical circuits.

In my patients with schizophrenia, I see what clearly appear to be information-processing problems, in which mundane random events are incorrectly viewed as parts of larger themes or patterns (an informational problem perhaps giving rise to paranoia and delusions). These patients also suffer from some failure of an internal "notification" mechanism that informs us when thoughts are self-generated (an informational problem perhaps underlying the frightening phenomenon of "hearing voices"). In my patients with autism spectrum disease, rather than inappropriately broad linkages in information, I see overly restricted information processing: they miss the big picture by focusing too narrowly on just parts of objects, people, conversations, and so on. These failures of information processing may lead to failures in communication and social behavior; better understanding of gamma oscillations may therefore provide insights into these complex diseases.

As a physician, I find this work thrilling because we are bringing engineering principles and quantitative technology to bear on devastating, seemingly "fuzzy" and intractable psychiatric diseases. Optogenetics is thus helping to move psychiatry toward a network-engineering approach, in which the complex functions of the brain (and the behaviors it produces) are interpreted as properties of the neural system that emerge from the electrochemical dynamics of the component cells and circuits. It thus fundamentally changes our understanding of how electrically excitable tissues function in health and disease. It has indeed been a long (and unpredictable) journey from marveling at the way a strange bacterial protein—bacteriorhodopsin—reacts to light.

Bounty of the Unexpected

At meetings of the Society for Neuroscience and some other very large conferences, I have occasionally heard colleagues suggest that it would be more efficient to focus tens of thousands of scientists on one massive and urgent project at a time—for example, Alzheimer's disease—rather than pursue more diverse explorations. Yet the more directed and targeted research becomes, the more likely we are to slow overall progress, and the more certain it is that the distant and untraveled realms of nature, where truly disruptive ideas can arise, will be utterly cut off from our common scientific journey.

The lesson of optogenetics is that the old, the fragile and the rare—even cells from pond scum or from harsh Saharan salt lakes—can be crucial to comprehension of ourselves and our modern world. The story behind this technology underscores the value of protecting rare environmental niches and the importance of supporting true basic science. We should never forget that we do not know where the long march of science is taking us or what will be needed to illuminate our path.

Does Optogenetics Challenge Ethics?

Optogenetics now joins the ranks of brain-modulation technologies, such as psychoactive drugs and surgical interventions, that are strong enough to raise ethical and philosophical questions. Yet if we look at it one way, optogenetics is actually safer and less fraught with ethical considerations than those older strategies. The increased power and specificity of optogenetics are coupled to its technological complexity: it would be virtually impossible to use optogenetics on an unwitting or unwilling patient.

More subtle (and perhaps more interesting) new issues arise from the precision of optogenetics, however. At some level, all aspects of our personalities, priorities, capabilities, emotions and memories arise from electrical and biochemical events within particular sets of neurons in particular temporal patterns. Controlling those key components of the mind would raise challenging philosophical questions, ranging from when it is appropriate or justifiable to make such modifications to more abstract questions about the very nature and modifiability of the self and the will.

Neural interventions based on surgery, drugs or electrodes have historically been so coarse that those important philosophical issues have been more theoretical than practical; ethicists and the law have only partially addressed them. The psychiatrist is no stranger to this type of question, given even our current medical capabilities to influence human emotions and the psychological construction of reality.

But times change, as the stunning rapidity of developments in optogenetics over the past few years exemplifies. Quantum leaps in the temporal and cellular precision of our interventions require ongoing and thoughtful consideration by society, as all advanced technologies do. Neuroscientists must therefore be prepared to explain carefully to the interested layperson what optogenetics experiments mean (and do not mean) for our understanding and treatment of the human mind.

About the Author

Karl Deisseroth is a professor of bioengineering and psychiatry at Stanford University. He was the recipient of the 2015 Lurie Prize in Biomedical Sciences for the development of CLARITY and optogenetics.

A Cell Atlas Reveals the Biodiversity inside Our Head

By Christof Koch, Hongkui Zeng, and Ed S. Lein

There are two fundamental theories in biology: Darwin's *theory of evolution* by natural selection and the *cell theory*, the observation that organismic life consists of one or more cells, the atoms of biology. Furthermore, all cells arise from previous cells by cell division, passing on their DNA source code in their genes in the process. Multicellular organisms have taken to this lifestyle with a vengeance, evolving into vast collections of highly diverse cellular communities that work together in a tightly coordinated manner across all organs in ways that escape our understanding and that make up a living being. A typical human body comprises an astounding 30 trillion cells (close in number to the dollars of the total U.S. debt), with fewer than 200 billion cells, under 1 percent, making up the central nervous system.

Focusing on the brain, microscopic observations by 19th-century anatomists provided the earliest description of distinct neurons that continue to be studied today: Betz neurons, Purkinje neurons, Meynert neurons and so on. The invention of dyes rendered their glorious complexity visible. The dyes stained with precision even cells' far-flung components—dendrites, the tiny, filamentlike signal-receiving antennae; cell bodies, the neurons' processing centers; and axons, the cells' output wires.

The hand-drawn sketches of Santiago Ramón y Cajal, the pioneering Spanish neuroanatomist, did much to establish the neuron doctrine for the brain. His drawings, exhibited at galleries the world over, gracing coffee-table books, T-shirts and the "inked" upper left arm of the first author (Koch), reveal the distinct nature of different cell types: Purkinje cells of the cerebellum with their coral-shaped dendritic trees; pyramidal cells of the cerebral cortex; and the layers of cells that tile the back of the eye.

Through such laborious anatomical investigations, it became clear that there are many types of neurons in the brain. Each region, such as the retina, spinal cord, cerebellum, thalamus and cerebral cortex, the outermost layer of the brain that gives rise to perception, memory, thought, consciousness and action, has its own specialized complement of cell types, all working together harmoniously. Just like in any advanced economy, it is all about differentiation and integration.

This makes the nervous system radically different from the architecture of integrated electronic circuits, in which a handful of specialized transistor types, arrayed on flat structures containing fields of tens of billions of transistors, can implement any possible computation. Of course, bodies and brains self-assemble from a single fertilized egg in a lengthy, unsupervised process that takes nine months in utero and does not end until two decades later in mature adulthood, while computers are fabricated in their static final form under the rigid rules of industrial quality control and quality assurance.

Exhaustively cataloguing all types of brain cells and characterizing their shapes, molecular constituents and input-to-output functions is of considerable academic and clinical interest. Many neurological diseases can be traced back to defects and vulnerabilities in specific types of cells. They include retinal blindness, such as retinitis pigmentosa and Leber congenital amaurosis; spinal muscular atrophy; Dravet syndrome (also known as severe myoclonic epilepsy of infancy); frontotemporal dementia; Alzheimer's disease; and amyotrophic lateral sclerosis (also known as Lou Gehrig's disease).

It is the need for such a cell inventory that prompted the U.S. BRAIN Initiative, under the leadership of the National Institutes of Health, to establish the Brain Initiative Cell Census Network (BICCN) in 2017. Its aims are to identify all the different types of cells that make up the mammalian brain. BICCN is a far-flung collaboration among top researchers at U.S. universities and not-for-profit research institutes, funded by numerous large grants, three of which are led by Mike Hawrylycz, as well as the two last authors (Lein and Zeng), all from the Allen Institute for Brain Science.

BICCN and a distinct international effort called the Human Cell Atlas, which seeks to classify cell types in all organs making up the human body, are predicated on a powerful molecular technology, single-cell RNA sequencing (scRNA-Seq), that has taken biology by storm.

Each cell carries within its nucleus the hereditary information that makes the organism what it is. Its DNA is a blueprint of how it will develop into its adult form. This is the organism's source code, durable and redundant. However, while cells in an organism generally carry the same source code, a retinal cell differs from a Purkinje cell thanks to the actual genes that are expressed, or turned on, in that cell. Active genes are transcribed in a highly regulated process into the cell's mRNA, its transcriptome (yes, the same type of mRNA that makes up the beating heart of mRNA COVID vaccines). Think of RNA as volatile code that is executed at run time that translates the source code into actions.

Based on ongoing refinements in the sensitivity of next-generation technology, single-cell RNA sequencing reads out the expression profiles of all genes being used in thousands of cells. That involves about 20,000 protein coding genes and other noncoding regions of the genome, although any given cell only uses a subset of these transcripts. These can then be grouped using clustering algorithms into discrete types. Single-cell RNA-sequencing is now the gold standard in biology and medicine, for surveys large and small, from freshly prepared samples to frozen and archived tissue across many species. Both the sequencing and the analysis tools and methods keep on improving and dropping in cost.

Single-cell RNA-sequencing can be combined with other modalities that reconstruct the dendritic tree or trace the path of the wirelike extensions from neurons' cell bodies called axons as they wind their way across the entire brain. Still other techniques record the electrical response of neurons responding to injections of electrical current. Together, this suite of technologies provides an unprecedented, detailed and comprehensive view of the structure and function of cells.

Carried out in a standardized and systematic manner across hundreds of thousands of cells, the massive BICCN effort surveys the lay of the land, building an atlas of cortical cell types and how they vary across three species: mouse, marmoset monkey (found in South America) and human. The first fruits of the BICCN are now out in a packet of 17 articles published simultaneously in the international scientific journal *Nature*. This trove of data and metadata is available to anyone using dedicated browsers and viewers to further accelerate the discoveries of therapies. It is a massive effort with hundreds of authors.

The bulk of these papers focus on a highly specialized region found in all mammals called the primary motor cortex or M1. It is a strip of tissue extending in a left-right direction across the cortex, just underneath the crown of the head. This region represents a topographic motor map of the various body parts controlled by the brain, from toes to feet to hands and so on all the way to lips and mouth. In humans, primary motor cortex is characterized by the presence of exceptionally large cells, named Betz cells after the Ukrainian anatomist who described them, cells that send their axons all the way down to the spinal cord.

BICCN computational scientists applied various clustering algorithms to the mRNA transcripts expressed in cells from M1 to classify the cells, identifying about 100 different cell types. That is, cells could be sorted into one of a hundred different bins, with different groups of genes shared within each type. Aligning these groups across the three species examined gives rise to a consensus taxonomical tree, a representation like the one we're familiar with from high-school biology textbooks when describing species. At the bottom are the leaves of this tree, 45 cell types conserved across the three species.

Depending on the amount of shared mRNA transcripts (ultimately, the shared executable code), M1 brain cells come in two broad varieties: neural and non-neural derived cells. The next split along the neural branch divides true neurons from glial cells. The group of eight glial and nonneural types includes oligodendrocytes, astrocytes and microglia cells, all critical to supporting and nurturing the neurons. The neuron group divides into 13 excitatory or glutamatergic and 24 inhibitory or GABAergic neuronal types, defined by the action they exert on their targets, either increasing or decreasing their propensity to be excited, that is firing action potentials.

GABAergic cells, in turn, are further divided up into six subclasses found throughout the depth of the cortical sheet, from the most superficial part (layer 1) all the way to its bottom (layer 6). They are also called local interneurons, as they tend to have a limited spatial reach, modulating and dampening the electrical activity of excitatory cells, most of which are so-called pyramidal neurons that send their output to regions beyond their local neighborhood.

Different glutamatergic excitatory neurons likewise segregate according to where they are located within the cortical sheet, that is, the layer in which their cell bodies are located (say, layer 2 versus layer 5) and where they send their information. They may send signals to other cortical regions, to the striatum, to the thalamus or to the spinal cord (gigantic Betz pyramidal cells, for example). Each cell's mRNA expresses the zip code of the regions their output is targeting. The molecular transcript specifies the destinations in the dense terminology familiar to neuroanatomists: intratelencephalic- and extratelencephalic-projecting neurons or cortico-thalamic-projecting neurons.

A novel feature of these studies is that they measured both gene expression, using scRNA-Seq, and the state of the cell's packaging material, or chromatin. The tighter the DNA is wrapped, the less likely a gene will be accessible to the transcriptional machinery—and this is measured using techniques called single-cell epigenomics. Perhaps not surprisingly, gene expression and gene regulatory architecture, reflected in the epigenomics data, are highly aligned. While the former provides insight into what genes are turned on, the latter, measuring the chromatin state of each cell, is more akin to the life history of the cell and, ultimately, its identity.

The question of how many naturally occurring elements make up the periodic table of chemistry has a precise answer: 92 (including byproducts of nuclear reactions). The question of how many types of brain cell types make up a brain does not. Given that each cell expresses thousands of different species of RNA molecules, it is always possible to discover finer and finer distinctions among cells. The underlying high-dimensional landscape is one of slowly changing gradients, on occasion interrupted by abrupt discontinuities, but no obvious periodic regularities. The situation may be analogous to the question of how many species exist.

Sure, by some measure, a Chihuahua and a Bernese mountain dog are both members of a single species, *canis familiaris*, but considering their coat, size and behavior, these two breeds could well be considered different species depending on the exact metric one adopts. And so it is with brain cells, which depend on the variant of scRNA-seq technology that measured the transcriptome and whether additional epigenetic, morphological, functional and other modality-specific criteria are used for the classification and exact parameter settings. But by all measures, even in M1 there are at least 50 cell types, with perhaps a few thousand types across the entire brain.

While many of the exact genes expressed in any one cell type differ among the three species, the overall similarities are astounding, with some types aligning one-to-one in all three species, even though the last common ancestor of mice, monkeys and people lived 60 million years ago. And yet, we will never have dinner conversation with a mouse or a monkey. It is the variation from these remarkable cross-species similarities that makes the difference. This includes not only minute differences in the genes expressed in the brains, but also the thousandfold increase in numbers of cells across these species. There is also variation in the way these genes are regulated and species-specific specialization in cell types. One of these *Nature* papers demonstrates that the mouse has three excitatory, glutamatergic cells in the upper layers of its cortex while humans have five.

Mammals evolved with a powerful mechanism, an extended cortical sheet of neurons and supporting cells, the most complex piece of active matter in the known universe, that made them the dominant group of vertebrates. Its detailed molecular architecture reflects, in a highly organized and lawful manner, its function.

Ed Lein and Hongkui Zeng were lead investigators on grants that produced the NIH Cell Census.

About the Authors

Christof Koch is meritorious investigator at the Allen Institute in Seattle and the chief scientist at the Tiny Blue Dot Foundation in Santa Monica, as well as author of the forthcoming Then I am Myself the World – What Consciousness is and How to Expand It *. He serves on* Scientific American's *board of advisers.*

Ed S. Lein is senior investigator at the Allen Institute for Brain Science and an affiliate professor in department of neurological surgery at the University of Washington.

Hongkui Zeng is executive vice president and director of the Allen Institute for Brain Science and an affiliate professor in department of biochemistry at the University of Washington.

"Mini Brains" Are Not like the Real Thing

By Karen Weintraub

The idea of scientists trying to grow brain tissue in a dish conjures up all sorts of scary mental pictures (cue the horror-movie music). But the reality of the research is quite far from that sci-fi vision—and always will be, say researchers in the field. In fact, a leader in this area of research, Arnold Kriegstein of the University of California, San Francisco, says the reality does not measure up to what some scientists make it out to be.

In a paper published on January 29 in *Nature*, Kriegstein and his colleagues identified which genes were active in 235,000 cells extracted from 37 different organoids and compared them with 189,000 cells from normally developing brains. The organoids—at times called "mini brains," to the chagrin of some scientists—are not a fully accurate representation of normal developmental processes, according to the study.

Brain organoids are made from stem cells that are transformed from one cell type to the another until they end up as neurons or other mature cells. But according to the *Nature* paper, they do not always fully complete this developmental process. Instead the organoids tend to end up with cells that have not fully transformed into new cell types—and they do not re-create the normal brain's organizational structure. Psychiatric and neurodevelopmental conditions—including schizophrenia and autism, respectively—and neurodegenerative diseases such as Alzheimer's are generally specific to particular cell types and circuits.

Many of the organoid cells showed signs of metabolic stress, the study demonstrated. When the team transplanted organoid cells into mice, their identity became "crisper," and they acted more like normal cells, Kriegstein says. This result suggests that the culture conditions under which such cells are grown does not match those of a normally developing brain, he adds. "Cellular stress is reversible," Kriegstein says. "If we can reverse it, we're likely to see the identity of cells improve significantly at the same time."

Brain organoids are getting better at recapitulating the activities of small clusters of neurons, says Kriegstein, who is a professor of neurology and director of the Eli & Edythe Broad Center for Regeneration Medicine and Stem Cell Research at U.C.S.F. Scientists often make organoids from the cells of people with different medical conditions to better understand those conditions. But some scientists may have gone too far in making claims about insights they have derived from patient-specific brain organoids. "I'd be cautious about that," Kriegstein says. "Some of those changes might reflect the abnormal gene expression of the cells and not actually reflect a true disease feature. So that's a problem for scientists to address."

A small ball of cells grown in a dish may be able to re-create some aspects of parts of the brain, but it is not intended to represent the entire brain and its complexity, several researchers have asserted. These organoids are no more sentient than brain tissue removed from a patient during an operation, one scientist has said.

Of course, models are never perfect. Although animal models have led to fundamental insights into brain development, researchers have sought out organoids, or organs-in-a-dish, precisely because of the limitations of extrapolating biological insights from another species to humans. Alzheimer's has been cured hundreds of times in mice but never in us, for instance.

"That said, the current models are already very useful in addressing some fundamental questions in human brain development," says Hongjun Song, a professor of neuroscience at the Perelman School of Medicine at the University of Pennsylvania, who was not involved in the new research. Using brain organoids, he adds, the Zika virus was recently shown to attack neural stem cells, causing a response that could explain why some babies exposed to Zika in utero develop unusually small brains.

Michael Nestor, a stem cell expert, who did not participate in the new study, says his own organoids are very helpful for identifying unusual activity in brain cells grown from people with autism. And he notes that they will eventually be useful for screening potential drugs.

Even though the models will always be a simplification, the organoid work remains crucial, says Paola Arlotta, chair of the department of stem cell and regenerative biology at Harvard University, who was also not involved in the *Nature* study. Neuropsychiatric pathologies and neurodevelopmental conditions are generally the result of a large number of genetic changes, which are too complex to be modeled in rodents, she says.

Sergiu Pasca, another leader in the field, says that the cellular stress encountered by Kriegstein and his team might actually be useful in some conditions, helping to create in a dish the kinds of conditions that lead to diseases of neurodegeneration, for instance. "What I consider the most exciting feature remains our ability to derive neural cells and glial cells in vitro, understanding their intrinsic program of maturation in a dish," says Pasca, an assistant professor at Stanford University, who was not part of the new paper.

The ability to improve cell quality when exposed to the environment of the mouse brain suggests that it may be possible to overcome some of the current limitations, Arlotta says. There is not yet a single protocol for making brain organoids in a lab, which may be for the best at this early stage of the field. Eventually, she says, scientists will optimize and standardize the conditions in which these cells are grown.

Arlotta, who is also the Golub Family Professor of Stem Cell and Regenerative Biology at Harvard, published a study last year in *Nature* showing that she and her colleagues can—over a six-month period—make organoids capable of reliably including a diversity of cell types that are appropriate for the human cerebral cortex. She says it is crucial for organoid work to be done within an ethical framework. Arlotta is part of a federally funded team of bioethicists and scientists working together to ensure that such studies proceed ethically. The scientists educate the bioethicists on the state of the research, she says, and the ethicists inform the scientists about the implications of their work.

Nestor feels so strongly about the importance of linking science, policy and public awareness around stem cell research that he has put his own laboratory at the Hussman Institute for Autism on hold to accept a year-long science-and-technology-policy fellowship with the American Association for the Advancement of Science. He says he took the post to make sure the public and policy makers understand what they need to know about organoids and other cutting-edge science and to learn how to communicate about science with them.

One thing all of the scientists interviewed for this article agree on is that these brain organoids are not actual mini brains, and no one is trying to build a brain in a dish. Even as researchers learn to make more cell types and grow them in more realistic conditions, they will never be able to replicate the brain's structure and complexity, Kriegstein says. "The exquisite organization of a normal brain is critical to its function," he adds. Brains are "still the most complicated structure that nature has ever created."

About the Author

Karen Weintraub is a staff writer at USA Today, *where she covers COVID, vaccine development and other health issues.*

The Fading Dream of the Computer Brain

By Noah Hutton

T welve years ago, when I graduated college, I was well aware of the Silicon Valley hype machine, but I considered the salesmanship of private tech companies a world away from objective truths about human biology I had been taught in neuroscience classes. At the time, I saw the neuroscientist Henry Markram proclaim in a TED talk that he had figured out a way to simulate an entire human brain on supercomputers within 10 years. This computer-simulated organ would allow scientists to instantly and noninvasively test new treatments for disorders and diseases, moving us from research that depends on animal experimentation and delicate interventions on living people to an "in silico" approach to neuroscience.

My 22-year-old mind didn't clock this as an overhyped proposal. Instead, it felt exciting and daring, the kind of moment that transforms a distant scientific pipe dream into a suddenly tangible goal and motivates funders and fellow researchers to think bigger. And so I began a 10-year documentary project following Markram and his Blue Brain Project, with the start of the film coinciding with the beginning of an era of big neuroscience where the humming black boxes produced by Silicon Valley came to be seen as the great new hope for making sense of the black boxes between our ears.

My decade-long journey documenting Markram's vision has no clear answers except perhaps one: that flashy presentations and sheer ambition are poor indicators of success when it comes to understanding the complex biological mechanisms of brains. Today, as we bear witness to a game of Pong being mind-controlled by a monkey as part of a typically bombastic demonstration by Elon Musk's start-up Neuralink, there is more of a need than ever to unwind the cycles of hype in order to grapple with what the future of brain technology and neuroscience have in store for humanity.

74

Hype of these sorts often relies on a selective amnesia for the unfulfilled promises of the past so that enthusiasm around scientific and technological progress can be replenished anew. My own initial excitement for the promises of the Blue Brain Project lingers with me, but has been folded into a messier, more complicated experience. The criticisms and technological limitations I encountered over the decade following Markram's TED talk have rendered each new neuro hype cycle into a potent reminder of those early enthusiasms and the danger of mishandling them.

My first shift in thinking occurred around three years into my time documenting the Blue Brain Project. Things weren't going as planned: there were magnificent fly-through visualizations of the first square millimeter of simulated rat brain set to *The Blue Danube* available in a visitor's screening room, but a definite lack of progress along the road map towards a human brain. Soon, there was talk of a necessary, larger endeavor known as the Human Brain Project that would require more money but would finally provide the resources necessary to achieve the goal. Proposals were submitted and the project won a billion euros in funding from the European Union, only to then be mired in controversy a year later after an open letter was signed by over 800 neuroscientists disagreeing with the core vision of how to simulate a human brain and objecting to the leadership style of its originator and director, Markram.

As scientific controversy and interpersonal fallout gradually made clear to me that the 10-year plan to recreate a human brain on a computer had perhaps been a pipe dream all along, I started to interview more critics of the endeavor, and began to examine in greater detail what it even meant to say you wanted to do such a thing. Princeton neuroscientist Sebastian Seung had posed a question to me during our interview that over time had come to vex me, pointing to scientific, ethical and moral pitfalls that this work was hurtling toward: "I would ask you this," Seung had begun, turning the question onto my own time so far filming at the Blue Brain Project and the nature of the piece of simulated mouse brain that project researchers had rendered in dazzling visualizations.

"They showed you a simulation of some neural activity inside this. Suppose it looked different; how would you know that that was wrong or right?" Sitting behind the camera, I replied, "Well, I wouldn't know." Seung reiterated: "Right, how would anybody know what was a wrong activity pattern or right activity pattern?"

The problems arrive when one begins to interrogate what "right" would entail in this situation, for recreating a profoundly noisy biological system inside the circuits of a perfectly programmed machine seems to eventually reach a fundamental platform issue. Biology runs on a motor of unpredictable "mistakes"—known as mutations—that generate the variability seen across individuals in a species and interact with our environment to drive evolutionary change through natural selection. Neurons are also known to be noisy elements, generating action potentials that are far from perfectly predictable events. In computers, on the other hand, structural mistakes, known as "bugs," are quickly fixed to make way for the perfect code for the task at hand.

Certainly, many elements of a human brain can be modeled, probed and have their generalities extracted, just as we've done for the human heart in order to create a device that could function in my body or yours, keeping us alive. But when it comes to building a full simulation of an individual human brain, which would "have a consciousness" and "would speak languages," as Markram had told me in our first interview, how would the determinate system of software running on computers ever capture the truly unpredictable mistakes seen at every level of biological life, from mutations in our DNA to the activity at a synapse?

Though the scientists I interviewed over the years shared a range of perspectives on the thorny issues of noise and chaos in computer simulations of biology, it wasn't until I conducted an interview with a more junior neuroscientist at the Blue Brain Project that I heard an answer that cut through the positivist public-relations gloss. Asked how one would ever find the "right" kind of variability in a simulation of a biological organism, she replied: "That's a good question, because the right kind, we can never know what's the right kind of variability."

If we can never know the right kind of variability, it seems that what we're really talking about in efforts to simulate biological structures on computers is a digital system that does exactly what its creators want it to do. Taking cues from AI, computational neuroscience is gradually leaving behind biological brains in search of perfect algorithms, which like its cousins in deep learning, may ultimately produce more black boxes that execute tasks but remain internally inscrutable.

In the halls of server farms and neuroscience labs intent on reproducing biological function on digital machines, ethical accountability for the identity of the simulation then becomes a central issue. Far from reaching an objective reconstruction of "the human brain," simulations of neural activity will ultimately hold a mirror up to the biases of their creators. And when it comes to tech companies that believe understanding a system is not essential to manipulating it or reproducing a version of it for profit, what will that mean when the system in question is the human brain?

One of Markram's motivations for wanting to accelerate neuroscience towards a full simulation of a human brain was the helplessness he felt when confronted by his son's autism diagnosis. Indeed, for many researchers in the field, the intentions behind the work can be deeply personal and, at least in theory, widely beneficial—which is why I remain drawn to the capability for improving the human condition enabled by experimentation and scientific ambition. Yet as technology races ahead and a certain strain of technocratic salesmanship continues to command the collective human ear, the line between fiction and reality will continue to be blurred, leading to cycles of hype and disappointment that threaten long-term public confidence in science.

This is an opinion and analysis article.

About the Author

Noah Hutton is a filmmaker, director and writer of the new documentary In Silico *and of the sci-fi feature* Lapsis.

Section 4: The Conscious Mind

4.1 How Our Brain Preserves Our Sense of Self
     By Robert Martone

4.2 A 25-Year-Old Bet about Consciousness Has Finally
     Been Settled
     By John Horgan

4.3 Some Patients Who 'Died' but Survived Report Lucid
     'Near-Death Experiences,' a New Study Shows
     By Rachel Nuwer

4.4 How the Mind Emerges from the Brain's
     Complex Networks
     By Max Bertolero and Dani S. Bassett

How Our Brain Preserves Our Sense of Self

By Robert Martone

We are all time travelers. Every day we experience new things as we travel forward through time. As we do, the countless connections among the nerve cells in our brain are recalibrated to accommodate these experiences. It's as if we reassemble ourselves daily, maintaining a mental construct of ourselves in physical time, and the glue that holds together our core identity is memory.

Our travels are not limited to physical time. We also experience mental time travel. We visit the past through our memories and then journey into the future by imagining what tomorrow or next year might bring. When we do so, we think of ourselves as we are now, remember who we once were and envision how we will be.

A study published in 2021 in the journal *Social Cognitive and Affective Neuroscience* (*SCAN*) explores how one particular brain region helps to knit together memories of the present and future self. When people sustain an injury to this area, it leads to an impaired sense of identity. The region—called the ventromedial prefrontal cortex (vmPFC)—may produce a fundamental model of the person and place it in mental time. When the region does so, this study suggests, it may be the source of our sense of self.

Psychologists have long noticed that a person's mind handles information about oneself differently from other details. Memories that reference the self are easier to recall than other forms of memory. They benefit from what researchers have called a self-reference effect, in which information related to oneself is privileged and more salient in that person's thoughts. Self-related memories are distinct from both episodic memory, the category of recollections that pertains to specific events and experiences, and semantic memory, which connects to more general knowledge, such as the color of grass and the characteristics of the seasons.

Self-reference effects, then, are a way to investigate how our sense of self emerges from the workings of the brain—something that multiple research groups have studied intensely. For example, previous research employed functional magnetic resonance imaging (fMRI), a method that uses blood flow and oxygen consumption in specific brain areas as a measure of neural activity, to identify regions that were activated by self-reference. These studies identified the medial prefrontal cortex (mPFC) as a brain region related to self-thought.

This area, the mPFC, can be further divided into upper and lower regions (called dorsal and ventral, respectively), and it turns out that each one makes different contributions to self-related thought. The dorsal section plays a role in distinguishing self from other and appears to be task-related, whereas the ventral section, the vmPFC, contributes more to emotional processing.

In the *SCAN* study, the researchers used the self-reference effect to assess memories of present and future selves among people who had brain lesions to the vmPFC. The scientists worked with seven people who had lesions to this area and then compared them with a control group made up of eight people with injuries to other parts of the brain, as well as 23 healthy individuals without brain injuries. By comparing these groups, the scientists could investigate whether brain lesions in general or those to the vmPFC specifically might affect self-reference. All people in the study underwent a thorough neuropsychological evaluation, which confirmed that they were within normal ranges for a variety of cognitive assessments, including measures of verbal fluency and spatial short-term memory. The researchers then asked the participants to list adjectives to describe themselves and a well-known celebrity, both in the present and 10 years in the future. Later, the participants had to recall these same traits.

The researchers discovered that people in their control group could recall more adjectives linked to themselves in the present and future than adjectives linked to the celebrity. In other words, scientists found that the self-reference effect extends to both the future and the present self. Although there was some variation in the group—people with brain injuries to areas other than the vmPFC were somewhat less able to recall details about their future self compared with noninjured participants—the self-reference effect still held true.

Results were distinctly different, however, for the participants with injuries to the vmPFC. People with lesions in this area had little or no ability to recall references to the self, regardless of the context of time. Their identification of adjectives for celebrities in the present or future was also significantly impaired compared with the rest of the participants' responses. In addition, people with vmPFC lesions had less confidence about an individual's ability to possess traits than other people in the study. All of this evidence points to a central role for the vmPFC in the formation and maintenance of identity.

These findings are intriguing for several reasons. Brain lesions can help us understand the normal function of the region involved. Lesions of the vmPFC are associated with altered personality, blunted emotions, and a number of changes in emotional and executive function. Injury to this area is most often associated with confabulations: false memories that people recite to listeners with great confidence. Although it may be tempting for someone to view confabulations as deliberate or creative falsehoods, people who tell them actually are unaware that their stories are false. Instead it is possible their confusion could stem from misfunctioning memory retrieval and monitoring mechanisms.

More broadly, the study helps us understand how self-related memories—recollections key to maintaining our core sense of identity—depend on the function of the vmPFC. But what about our past selves? Curiously, in previous studies that asked people to consider their past selves, there was no more activation of the mPFC than when considering someone else. Our past selves seem foreign to us, as if they were individuals apart from us.

One idea that scientists have put forward to understand this distinction is that perhaps we are not very kind in our judgments of our past selves. Instead we may be rather critical and harshly judgmental of our previous behavior, emotions and personal traits. In these situations, we may use our past primarily to construct a more positive self-image in the present. Put another way, because we may recognize flaws in our past self's behavior, we tend to distance ourselves from the person we once were.

Bringing the present and future into the spotlight, then, is central to understanding the way our brain and thoughts shape our current identities. In many ways, it makes sense that the mPFC is key in this process of recalling present details and imagining future ones that build on our memories. The prefrontal cortex, including the mPFC and its subdivisions, forms a network in the brain that is involved in future planning.

That network also includes the hippocampus, a brain structure that is central to episodic memory formation and that can track moments as sequential events in time. In earlier work, researchers found that manipulating the activity of the hippocampus alters creative and future imaginings, which suggests an important role for brain structures supporting memory in imagining the future. In fact, although we often think of memory as the brain's accurate and dispassionate recording device, some scholars have characterized it as a form of imagination.

Future thought is a vital component of being human. Its importance in our culture is embodied in the mythological figure and pre-Olympian god Prometheus (whose name means "forethinker"), patron of the arts and sciences. According to Greek legend, he shaped humans out of clay and bestowed them with fire and the skills of craftsmanship. These are acts that illustrate the power of imagining a novel future. Although there is debate as to whether thinking about the future is an exclusively human feature—birds such as Western Scrub-Jays, for example, appear to anticipate and plan for future food needs—it is clear that future thought has played a significant role in human evolution. This ability may have contributed to the development of language, and it has a key part in human interactions, where the vmPFC is central to evaluating and taking advantage of social context.

Now, thanks to this research, we have a better idea than ever about the way a small region within our brain is able to build and hold this core ability to maintain our identity.

About the Author

Robert Martone is a research scientist with expertise in neurodegeneration. He spends his free time kayaking and translating Renaissance Italian literature.

A 25-Year-Old Bet about Consciousness Has Finally Been Settled

By John Horgan

A neuroscientist clad in gold and red and a philosopher sheathed in black took the stage before a packed, murmuring auditorium at New York University on Friday night. The two men were grinning, especially the philosopher. They were here to settle a bet made in the late 1990s on one of science's biggest questions: How does a brain, a lump of matter, generate subjective conscious states such as the blend of anticipation and nostalgia I felt watching these guys?

Before I reveal their bet's resolution, let me take you through its twisty backstory, which reveals why consciousness remains a topic of such fascination and frustration to anyone with even the slightest intellectual leaning. I first saw Christof Koch, the neuroscientist, and David Chalmers, the philosopher, butt heads in 1994 at a now legendary conference in Tucson, Ariz., called "Toward a Scientific Basis for Consciousness." Koch was a star of the meeting. Together with biophysicist Francis Crick, he had been proclaiming in *Scientific American* and elsewhere that consciousness, which philosophers have wrestled with for millennia, was scientifically tractable.

Just as Crick and geneticist James Watson solved heredity by decoding DNA's double helix, scientists would crack consciousness by discovering its neural underpinnings, or "correlates." Or so Crick and Koch claimed. They even identified a possible basis for consciousness: brain cells firing in synchrony 40 times per second.

Not everyone in Tucson was convinced. Chalmers, younger and then far less well known than Koch, argued that neither 40-hertz oscillations nor any other strictly physical process could account for why perceptions are accompanied by conscious sensations, such as the crushing boredom evoked by a jargony lecture. I have a vivid memory of the audience perking up when Chalmers called consciousness "the hard problem." That was the first time I heard that now famous phrase.

Chalmers suggested that the hard problem might be solved by assuming that "information" is a fundamental property of reality. This hypothesis, unlike Crick and Koch's 40-hertz model, could account for consciousness in *any* system, not just one with a brain. Even a thermostat, which processes a little information, might be a little conscious, Chalmers speculated.

Unimpressed, Koch confronted Chalmers at a cocktail reception and denounced his information hypothesis as untestable and hence pointless. "Why don't you just say that when you have a brain, the Holy Ghost comes down and makes you conscious?" Koch grumbled.

Chalmers replied coolly that the Holy Ghost hypothesis conflicted with his own subjective experience. "But how do I know that your subjective experience is the same as mine?" Koch exclaimed. "How do I even know you're conscious?" Koch was implicitly raising what I call the solipsism problem, to which I will return.

I highlighted the clash between Koch and Chalmers in a 1994 article for *Scientific American*, "Can Science Explain Consciousness?" I've been tracking their careers ever since. Their views hadn't changed much when they made their wager in 1998 at the annual meeting of the Association for the Scientific Study of Consciousness, which they helped establish. Koch bet Chalmers a case of wine that within 25 years—that is, by 2023—researchers would discover a "clear" neural pattern underlying consciousness.

Over the next decade, however, Koch's position shifted dramatically, as he embraced an ambitious information-based model invented by neuroscientist Giulio Tononi. Called integrated information theory, or IIT, the model is much more detailed than the one Chalmers sketched out in Tucson. IIT holds that consciousness arises in any system whose components swap information in a certain mathematically defined way.

In 2009 Koch spelled out the theory's startling implications in *Scientific American*. A single proton, which consists of three interacting quarks, might possess a glimmer of consciousness, he conjectured.

IIT seemed to corroborate the ancient metaphysical doctrine of panpsychism, which holds that consciousness pervades everything.

Perplexed by these claims, in 2015 I attended a workshop on integrated information theory at N.Y.U. The speakers included Tononi, IIT's inventor, Koch, now director of the Allen Institute for Brain Science, and Chalmers, co-director of N.Y.U.'s Center for Mind, Brain and Consciousness.

Although most speakers at the workshop treated IIT gently, quantum computing expert Scott Aaronson eviscerated it. According to IIT's mathematical definition of information, Aaronson pointed out, a compact disc player running error-correction codes can be far more conscious than a human being.

I came away from the workshop with more basic objections to IIT. In a 1990 interview Claude Shannon, who invented information theory in the 1940s, told me that the information in a system is proportional to its capacity to "surprise" an observer, which I take to mean that information requires a conscious entity to be informed. Explaining consciousness with a concept that presupposes consciousness strikes me as circular reasoning—cheating.

Moreover IIT, like all theories that allow for nonhuman consciousness, poses what I referred to above as the solipsism problem: no human can be sure that any other *human* is conscious, let alone a jellyfish, thermostat or proton. Koch has proposed building a "consciousness meter" that would measure consciousness in any object in the same way that a thermometer measures temperature, but this device remains a thought experiment, a fantasy.

So where do things stand today? Thanks in part to the efforts of Koch and Chalmers, more researchers than ever are trying to solve the conundrum of consciousness. They are probing the brain with optogenetics, functional magnetic resonance imaging, transcranial magnetic stimulation and electrodes implanted inside brains. And they are modeling their data with ever more powerful, artificial-intelligence-augmented algorithms.

These efforts were showcased at the 26th annual conference of the Association for the Scientific Study of Consciousness at N.Y.U., where Koch and Chalmers met to settle their bet. At the June 22–25 gathering, scores of researchers from all over the world, some unborn when Koch and Chalmers first clashed in Tucson, presented their latest ideas and data.

The diversity of perspectives was dizzying. The old 40-hertz oscillation hypothesis of Crick and Koch has yielded to a welter of fancier neural-correlate models. In some, the prefrontal cortex is essential to consciousness; others focus on activity in different regions of the brain or involving specific types of neuron or modes of neural communication. Speakers also delved into the consciousness of primates, spiders and plants, the ontological status of virtual reality and dreams and the implications of dementia and other pathological states.

One topic that was conspicuously absent was quantum mechanics, which physicists such as John Wheeler and Roger Penrose have linked to consciousness. Chalmers has recently toyed with a model that fuses integrated information theory and quantum mechanics. But when I asked Chalmers about the omission of quantum theories of consciousness, he informed me that they were too fringy for this conference.

So quantum theories were beyond the pale. But what about the poster on how consciousness can be explained by relativity, which provides a way to unite first-person and third-person frames of reference? What about the session that considered whether artificial intelligences such as ChatGPT are conscious and hence morally responsible? What about the talks on mystical experiences induced by meditation, DMT and LSD?

Speakers fretted over the proliferation of theories. "Growth is not always benign," said philosopher Robert Chis-Ciure in a talk on falsification of theories. "Cancer is a good example." During the same evening event at which Koch and Chalmers settled their bet, researchers presented the results of rigorous tests of integrated information theory and a rival model, the global workspace theory, in which consciousness serves as the brain's way of spotlighting critical information.

The results of the tests were inconclusive. Some data favor IIT; others favor the global workspace. This conclusion is hardly surprising, given that the brain is so hideously complex and that consciousness is so poorly defined, as multiple speakers acknowledged. All of this is to say that consciousness research, far from converging toward a unifying paradigm, has become more fractious and chaotic than ever.

Back to the bet between Koch and Chalmers: They agreed that, for Koch to win, the evidence for a neural signature of consciousness must be "clear." That word "clear" doomed Koch. "It's clear that things are not clear," Chalmers said, and Koch, grimacing, concurred. He stalked off the stage and reappeared with a case of wine as the audience laughed and applauded.

Koch then doubled down on his bet. Twenty-five years from now, he predicted, when he will be age 91 and Chalmers will be age 82, consciousness researchers will achieve the "clarity" that now eludes them. Chalmers, shaking Koch's hand, took the bet.

"I hope I lose," Chalmers said, "but I suspect I'll win." I suspect so, too. I bet consciousness will be even more baffling in 2048 than it is today. I hope to live long enough to see Koch give Chalmers another case of wine.

About the Author

John Horgan, who has written for Scientific American *since 1986, comments on science on his free online journal* Cross-Check. *He has also posted his books* Mind-Body Problems *and* My Quantum Experiment *online. Horgan teaches at Stevens Institute of Technology.*

Some Patients Who "Died" but Survived Report Lucid "Near-Death Experiences," a New Study Shows

By Rachel Nuwer

What happens when we actually die—when our heart stops and all electrical activity "flatlines" in our brain?

Humans have been asking this question since time immemorial. It's a tough one because the dead do not normally ping back to us about the nature of their experiences. Religious texts are capable of supplying a multitude of explanations. But scientists have not given up on providing their own set of answers, and they are making some strides in better understanding the brain's process of transitioning from life to death.

Most recently, this has become possible because of research that has monitored the brains of people who have been in the throes of actually dying. Some of these individuals have been able to report back about what they experienced. According to findings published on September 14 in *Resuscitation*, the flatlined brains of some cardiac arrest patients burst into a flurry of activity during CPR, even though their heart stopped beating up to an hour. A small subset of study participants who survived were able to recall the experience, and one person was able to identify an audio stimulus that was played while doctors were trying to resuscitate them.

The researchers interpret the brain recordings they made of these patients as markers of "lucid, recalled experiences of death"—an observation that has "never been possible before," says lead author Sam Parnia, an associate professor of medicine at NYU Langone Health and a longtime researcher of what happens to people as they die. "We've also been able to put forward a coherent, mechanistic explanation for why this occurs."

"Recalled experiences of death"—a term Parnia prefers over "near-death experiences" for accuracy—have been reported across diverse cultures throughout recorded history. Some Western scientists previously dismissed such stories as hallucinations or dreams, but recently a few research teams have begun to pay more serious attention to the phenomena as a means to investigate consciousness and shine light on the mysteries of death.

In the new study, Parnia and his colleagues sought to find a biological signature of recalled experiences of death. They teamed up with 25 hospitals, primarily in the U.S. and the U.K. Medical personnel used portable devices that could be placed on the heads of patients who were having a cardiac emergency to measure their brain oxygen levels and electrical activity without interfering with their medical treatment. The researchers also tested for conscious and unconscious perceptions by placing headphones on patients that played a repeated recording of the names of three fruits: banana, pear and apple. In terms of unconscious learning, a person who does not remember hearing these fruit names but is asked to "randomly think of three fruits" may still give the right answer, Parnia says. Past research has shown, for example, that even people in a deep coma can unconsciously learn the names of fruits or cities if those words are whispered in their ear.

Between May 2017 and March 2020, 567 people suffered cardiac arrests at participating hospitals. Medical staff managed to gather usable brain oxygen and activity data from 53 of these patients, most of whom showed an electrical flatline state on electroencephalographic (EEG) brain monitors. But about 40 percent then experienced electrical activity that reemerged at some point with normal to near-normal brain waves that were consistent with consciousness. This activity was sometimes restored up to 60 minutes into CPR.

Of the 567 total patients, just 53 survived. The researchers conducted interviews with 28 of the survivors. They also interviewed 126 people from the community who had gone through cardiac arrests because the sample size of survivors from the new study was so small. Nearly 40 percent reported some perceived awareness of the event without specific memories attached, and 20 percent seemed to have had a recalled experience of death. Many in the latter group described the event as a "moral evaluation" of "their entire life and how they've conducted themselves," Parnia says.

In their interviews with survivors, the researchers found that just one person was able to recall the names of fruits that had been played while they received CPR. Parnia acknowledges that this individual could have guessed the correct fruits by chance.

He and his colleagues have developed a working hypothesis to explain their findings. Normally, the brain has "braking systems" in place that filter most elements of brain function out of our experience of consciousness. This enables people to efficiently operate in the world, because under regular circumstances, "you couldn't function with access to your whole brain's activity being in the realm of consciousness," he says.

In the dying brain, however, the researchers hypothesize that the braking system is removed. Parts that are normally dormant become active, and the dying person gains access to their entire consciousness—"all your thoughts, all your memories, everything that's been stored before," Parnia says. "We don't know the evolutionary benefit of this, but it seems to prepare people for their transition from life into death."

The findings also raise questions about the brain's resiliency to oxygen deprivation. It could be, Parnia says, that some people who have conventionally been thought to be beyond the point of saving could in fact be revived. "The traditional thinking among doctors is that the brain, once deprived of oxygen for five to 10 minutes, dies," he says. "We were able to show that the brain is quite robust in terms of its ability to resist oxygen deprivation for prolonged periods of time, which opens up new pathways for finding treatments for brain damage in the future."

The new study "represents a Herculean effort to understand as objectively as possible the nature of brain function as it may apply to consciousness and near-death experiences during cardiac arrest," says Lakhmir Chawla, an intensive care unit physician at Jennifer Moreno Department of Veterans Affairs Medical Center in San Diego, Calif., who was not involved in the research but has published papers on spikes of EEG activity at the time of death in some patients.

While the results Parnia and his colleagues report are "striking" from a scientific point of view, "I believe that we should allow these data to also inform our humanity," he adds. For one, the findings should "compel clinicians to treat patients who are receiving CPR as if they are awake," which is something "we rarely do."

And for those individuals who do seem to be beyond saving, Chawla says, doctors could invite their families in to come say goodbye, "as the patient may still be able to hear them."

About the Author

Rachel Nuwer is a freelance science journalist and author who regularly contributes to Scientific American, *the* New York Times *and* National Geographic, *among other publications. Follow Nuwer on X (formerly Twitter) @RachelNuwer*

How the Mind Emerges from the Brain's Complex Networks

By Max Bertolero and Dani S. Bassett

Networks pervade our lives. Every day we use intricate networks of roads, railways, maritime routes and skyways traversed by commercial flights. They exist even beyond our immediate experience. Think of the World Wide Web, the power grid and the universe, of which the Milky Way is an infinitesimal node in a seemingly boundless network of galaxies. Few such systems of interacting connections, however, match the complexity of the one underneath our skull.

Neuroscience has gained a higher profile in recent years, as many people have grown familiar with splashily colored images that show brain regions "lighting up" during a mental task. There is, for instance, the temporal lobe, the area by your ear, which is involved with memory, and the occipital lobe at the back of your head, which dedicates itself to vision.

What has been missing from this account of human brain function is how all these distinct regions interact to give rise to who we are. We and other researchers have drawn on a branch of mathematics called graph theory to better parse, probe and predict complex interactions in the brain that bridge the seemingly vast gap between frenzied neural electrical activity and an array of cognitive tasks—sensing, remembering, making decisions, learning a new skill and initiating movement. This new field of network neuroscience builds on and reinforces the idea that certain regions of the brain carry out defined activities. In the most fundamental sense, what the brain is—and thus who we are as conscious beings—is, in fact, defined by a sprawling network of 100 billion neurons with at least 100 trillion connecting points, or synapses.

Network neuroscience seeks to capture this complexity. We can now model the data supplied by brain imaging as a graph composed of nodes and edges. In a graph, nodes represent the units of the network, such as neurons or, in another context, airports. Edges serve as the connections between nodes—think of one neuron intertwined with the next, or contemplate airline flight routes. In our work, we reduce the human brain to a graph of roughly 300 nodes. Diverse areas can be linked together by edges representing the brain's structural connections: thick bundles of tubular wires called white matter tracts that tie together brain regions. This depiction of the brain as a unified network has already furnished a clearer picture of cognitive functioning, along with the practical benefit of enabling better diagnoses and treatment of psychiatric disorders. In the future, an understanding of brain networks may lead to a blueprint for improved artificial intelligence, new medicines, electrical-stimulation technology to alter malfunctioning neural circuitry in people with depression— and perhaps even the development of genetic therapies to treat mental illness.

The Music of the Mind

To understand how networks underlie our cognitive capabilities, first consider the analogy of an orchestra playing a symphony. Until recently, neuroscientists have largely studied the functioning of individual brain regions in isolation, the neural equivalent of separate brass, percussion, string and woodwind sections. In the brain, this categorization represents an approach that dates back to Plato—quite simply, it entails carving nature at the joints and then studying the individual components that remain.

Just as it is useful to understand how the amygdala helps to process emotions, it is similarly vital to grasp how a violin produces high-pitched sounds. Still, even a complete list of brain regions and their functions—vision, motor, emotion, and so on—does not tell us how the brain really works. Nor does an inventory of instruments provide a recipe for Beethoven's *Eroica* symphony.

Network neuroscientists have begun to probe these mysteries by examining the way each brain region is embedded in a larger network of such regions and by mapping the connections between regions to study how each fits into the large, integrated network that is the brain. There are two major approaches. First, examining structural connectivity captures the instrumentation of the brain's orchestra. It is the physical means of creating the music, and the unique instrumentation of a given musical work constrains what can be played. Instrumentation matters, but it is not the music itself. Put another way, just as a collection of instruments is not music, an assemblage of wires does not represent brain function.

Second, living brains are massive orchestras of neurons that fire together in quite specific patterns. We hear a brain's music by measuring the correlation between the activity of each pair of regions, which indicates that they are working in concert. This measure of joint activity is known as functional connectivity, and we colloquially think of it as reflecting the music of the brain. If two regions fire with the same time-varying fluctuations, they are considered as functionally connected. This music is just as important as the decibels produced by a French horn or a viola. The volume of the brain's music can be thought of as the level of activity of electrical signals buzzing about one brain area or another.

At any moment, though, some areas within the three-pound organ are more active than others. We have all heard that people use a small fraction of their brain capacity. In fact, the entire brain is active at any point in time, but a given task modulates the activity of only a portion of the brain from its baseline level of activity.

That arrangement does not mean that you fulfill only half of your cognitive potential. In fact, if your entire brain were strongly active at the same time, it would be as if all the orchestra members were playing as loudly as possible—and that scenario would create chaos, not enable communication. The deafening sound would not convey the emotional overtones present in a great musical piece. It is the pitch, rhythms, tempo and strategic pauses that communicate information, both during a symphony and inside your head.

Modularity

Just as an orchestra can be divided into groups of instruments from different families, the brain can be separated into collections of nodes called modules—a description of localized networks. All brains are modular. Even the 302-neuron network of the nematode *Caenorhabditis elegans* has a modular structure. Nodes within a module share stronger connections to one another than to nodes in other modules.

Each module in the brain has a certain function, just as every family of instruments plays a role in the symphony. We recently carried out an evaluation of a large number of independent studies—a meta-analysis—that included more than 10,000 functional magnetic resonance imaging (fMRI) experiments of subjects performing 83 different cognitive tasks and discovered that separate tasks map to different brain-network modules. There are modules occupied with attention, memory and introspective thought. Other modules, we found, are dedicated to hearing, motor movement and vision.

These sensory and motor cognitive processes involve single, contiguous modules, most of which are confined to one lobe of the brain. We also found that computations in modules do not spur more activity in other modules—a critical aspect of modular processing. Imagine a scenario in which every musician in an orchestra had to change the notes played every time another musician changed their notes. The orchestra would spiral out of control and would certainly not produce aesthetically pleasing sounds. Processing in the brain is similar—each module must be able to function mostly independently. Philosophers as early as Plato and as recent as Jerry Fodor have noted this necessity, and our research confirms it.

Even though brain modules are largely independent, a symphony requires that families of instruments be played in unison. Information generated by one module must eventually be integrated with other modules. Watching a movie with only a brain module for vision—without access to the one for emotions—would detract greatly from the experience.

For that reason, to complete many cognitive tasks, modules must often work together. A short-term memory task—holding a new phone number in your head—requires the cooperation of auditory, attention and memory-processing modules. To integrate and control the activity of multiple modules, the brain uses hubs—nodes where connections from the brain's different modules meet.

Some key modules that control and integrate brain activity are less circumspect than others in their doings. Their connections extend globally to multiple brain lobes. The frontoparietal control module spans the frontal, parietal and temporal lobes. It developed relatively recently on the timescale of evolution. The module is especially large in humans, relative to those of our closest primate ancestors. It is analogous to an orchestra conductor and becomes active across a large number of cognitive tasks.

The frontoparietal module ensures that the brain's multiple modules function in unison. It is heavily involved in what is called executive function, which encompasses the separate processes of decision-making, short-term memory and cognitive control. The last is the ability to develop complex strategies and inhibit inappropriate behavior.

Another highly interconnected module is the salience module, which hooks up to the frontoparietal control module and contributes to a range of behaviors related to attention and responses to novel stimuli. For example, take a look at two words: blue and red. If you are asked to tell someone the color of the words, you will react much faster to the one set in red. For the one set in green, your frontoparietal and salience modules activate when responding to its color because you have to suppress a natural inclination to answer "blue."

Finally, the default mode module spans the same lobes as the frontoparietal control network. It contains many hubs and is linked to a variety of cognitive tasks, including introspective thought, learning, memory retrieval, emotional processing, inference of the mental state of others, and even gambling. Critically, damage to these hub-rich modules disturbs functional connections throughout the brain and causes widespread cognitive difficulties, just as bad weather at a hub airport delays air traffic all over the country.

Personal Connections

Although our brains have certain basic network components—modules interconnected by hubs—each of us shows slight variations in the way our neural circuits are wired. Researchers have devoted intense scrutiny to this diversity. In an initial phase of what is called the Human Connectome Project, 1,200 young people volunteered for a study of brain-network architecture, funded by the National Institutes of Health. (The final goal of the project is to map connectomes across the entire life span.) Each individual's structural and functional connectivity networks were probed using fMRI. These data were supplemented by a battery of testing and questionnaires to analyze 280 behavioral and cognitive traits. Participants provided information about how well they slept, how often they drank alcohol, their language and memory abilities, and their emotional states. Neuroscientists from all over the world have pored over this incredibly rich data set to learn how our brain networks encode who we are.

Using data from hundreds of participants in the Human Connectome Project, we and others have demonstrated that brain-connectivity patterns establish a "fingerprint" that distinguishes each individual. People with strong functional connections among certain regions have an extensive vocabulary, exhibit higher fluid intelligence—helpful for solving novel problems—and are able to delay gratification. They tend to have more education and life satisfaction, as well as better memory and attention. People with weaker functional connections among those same brain areas have lower fluid intelligence, histories of substance use, poor sleep and a decreased capacity for concentration.

Inspired by this research, we showed that the findings could be described by particular patterns among the hub connections. If your brain network has strong hubs with many connections across modules, it tends to have modules that are clearly segregated from one another, and you will perform better on a range of tasks, from short-term memory to mathematics, language or social cognition. Put simply, your thoughts, feelings, quirks, flaws and mental strengths are all encoded by the specific organization of the brain as a unified, integrated network. In sum, it is the music your brain plays that makes you you.

The brain's synchronized modules both establish your identity and help to retain it over time. The musical compositions they play appear to always be similar. The likeness could be witnessed when participants in two other studies in the Human Connectome Project engaged in various tasks that involved short-term memory, recognition of the emotions of others, gambling, finger tapping, language, mathematics, social reasoning and a self-induced "resting state" in which they let their mind wander.

Fascinatingly, the networks' functional wiring has more similarities than expected across all these activities. Returning to our analogy, it is not as if the brain plays Beethoven when doing math and Tupac when resting. The symphony in our head comes from the same musician playing the same musical genre. This consistency derives from the fact that the brain's physical pathways, or structural connections, place constraints on the routes over the brain's integrated network that a neural signal can travel. And those pathways delineate how functional connections— the ones, say, for math or language—can be configured. In the music metaphor, a bass drum cannot play the melodic line of a piano.

Changes in the brain's music inevitably occur, just as new arrangements do for orchestral music. Physical connections undergo alterations over the course of months or years, whereas functional connectivity shifts on the order of seconds when a person switches between one mental task and the next.

Transformations in both structural and functional connectivity are important during adolescent brain development, when the finishing touches of the brain's wiring diagram are being refined.

This period is of critical importance because the first signs of mental disorders often appear in adolescence or early adulthood.

One area our research relates to is understanding how brain networks develop through childhood and adolescence and into adulthood. These processes are driven by underlying physiological changes, but they are also influenced by learning, exposure to new ideas and skills, an individual's socioeconomic status, and other experiences.

Brain-network modules emerge very early in life, even in the womb, but their connectivity is refined as we grow up. Consistent strengthening of the structural connections to hubs throughout the course of childhood is associated with an increase in the segregation between modules and augmentation of the efficiency with which young people perform executive tasks such as complex reasoning and self-regulation. We have also found that the segregation of modules from one another is more rapid in children who have a higher socioeconomic status, highlighting the key impact of their environment.

Although changes in structural connectivity are slow, the reconfiguration of functional connections can occur quickly, within a few seconds or minutes. These rapid shifts are instrumental for moving between tasks and for the massive amount of learning demanded by even a single task. In a set of studies that we published from 2011 to 2019, we found that networks with modules that can change readily turn up in individuals who have greater executive function and learning capacity.

To better understand what was happening, we used publicly available data from a landmark study known as MyConnectome, in which Stanford University psychology professor Russell Poldrack personally underwent imaging and cognitive appraisals three times a week for more than a year. Although modules are mostly autonomous and segregated, at times the brain will spontaneously reorganize its connections. This property, called functional network flexibility, lets a node with strong functional connections within a module suddenly establish many connections to a different module, changing the flow of information through the network. Using data from this study, we found that the rerouting of a network's connections changes from day to day in a manner that matches positive mood, arousal and fatigue. In healthy individuals, such network flexibility correlates with better cognitive function.

Dissonant Notes

The configuration of brain connections also reflects one's mental health. Aberrant connectivity patterns accompany depression, schizophrenia, Alzheimer's, Parkinson's, autism spectrum disorder, attention deficit disorder, dementia and epilepsy.

Most mental illnesses are not confined to one area of the brain. The circuitry affected in schizophrenia extends quite widely across the entire organ. The so-called disconnectivity hypothesis for schizophrenia holds that there is nothing abnormal about the individual modules. Instead the disarray relates to an overabundance of connections between modules.

In a healthy brain, modules are mostly autonomous and segregated, and the ability to bring about flexible changes in network connections is beneficial for cognitive functioning—within certain limits. In our research, we found that in the brains of people with schizophrenia and their first-degree relatives, there is an overabundance of flexibility in how networks reconfigure themselves. Auditory hallucinations might result when nodes unexpectedly switch links between speech and auditory modules. The uninvited mix can result in what seem to be the utterings of voices in one's head.

Like schizophrenia, major depressive disorder is not caused by a single abnormal brain region. Three specific modules appear to be affected in depression: the frontoparietal control, salience and default mode modules. In fact, the symptoms of depression—emotional disinhibition, altered sensitivity to emotional events and rumination—map to these modules.

As a result, normal communication among the three modules becomes destabilized. Activities from module to module typically tug back and forth to balance the cognitive processing of sensory inputs with more introspective thoughts. In depression, though, the default mode dominates, and the afflicted person lapses into ruminative thought. The music of the brain thus becomes increasingly unbalanced, with one family of instruments governing the symphony. These observations have broadened our understanding of the network properties of depression to the extent that a connectivity pattern in a brain can allow us to diagnose certain subtypes of the disorder and determine which areas should be treated with electrical-stimulation technology.

Networks Evolve

Besides studying development, network neuroscientists have begun to ask why brain networks have taken their present form over tens of thousands of years. The areas identified as hubs are also the locations in the human brain that have expanded the most during evolution, making them up to 30 times the size they are in macaques. Larger brain hubs most likely permit greater integration of processing across modules and so support more complex computations. It is as if evolution increased the number of musicians in a section of the orchestra, fostering more intricate melodies.

Another way neuroscientists have explored these questions is by creating computer-generated networks and subjecting them to evolutionary pressures. We have probed the evolutionary origins of hubs. This exercise started with a network in which all edges were placed uniformly at random. Next, the network was rewired, mimicking natural selection to form segregated modules and display a property known in network science as small-worldness, in which paths form to let distant network nodes communicate with surprising ease. Thousands of such networks then evolved, each of which ultimately contained hubs strongly connected to multiple modules but also tightly interconnected to one another, forming what is called a club. Nothing in the selection process explicitly selected for a club of hubs—they simply emerged from this iterative process.

This simulation demonstrates that one potential path to evolving a brain capable of exchanging information among modules requires hubs with strong connections. Notably, real networks—brains, airports, power grids—also have durable, tightly interconnected hubs, exactly as predicted by evolutionary experiments. That observation does not mean evolution necessarily occurred in the same way as the simulation, but it shows a possible means by which one of nature's tricks might operate.

States of Mind

When Nobel Prize–winning physicist Richard Feynman died in 1988, his blackboard read, "What I cannot create, I do not understand." He created a beautiful aphorism, yet it misses a pivotal idea: it should be revised to "What I cannot create *and control,* I do not understand." Absent such control, we still know enough to enjoy a symphony, even if we do not qualify to be the conductor.

When it comes to the brain, we have a basic understanding of its form and the importance of its network architecture. We know that our brain determines who we are, but we are just beginning to understand how it all happens. To rephrase mathematician Pierre-Simon Laplace's explanation of determinism and mechanics and apply it to the brain, one's present brain, and so one's mental state, can be thought of as a compilation of past states that can be used to predict the future. A neuroscientist who knew all the principles of brain function and everything about someone's brain could predict that person's mental conditions—the future, as well as the past, would be present inside the person's mind.

This knowledge could be used to prevent pain and suffering, given that many mental illnesses are associated with network abnormalities. With enough engineering ingenuity, we may develop implanted devices that alter brain networks or even generate new ones to prevent the disorganization associated with mental disorders from occurring in the first place. Such an achievement would enable us to treat diseases and help to restore brain function after stroke or injury or, potentially, enhance function in healthy individuals.

Before those futuristic scenarios materialize, two major gaps must be filled: we need to know more about how personal genetics, early-life development and environment determine one's brain's structure and how that structure leads to functional capacities. Neuroscientists have some knowledge from the human genome about the structure that gives rise to functional networks but still need to learn precisely how this process occurs. We are starting to grasp the way brain networks develop and are shaped by the environment, but we are not close to explaining the entire complexity of this process. The brain's wiring, its structural connectivity, constrains how various modules interact with one another, but our knowledge remains limited. As we fill in these gaps, chances improve for interventions to guide brain functioning into healthy trajectories.

What holds us back, for the moment, is our still blurry vision of the brain—it is as if we are outside the concert hall and have seen only sketches of the instruments. Inside each brain region that neuroscientists study are millions of neurons firing every millisecond, and we are able just to indirectly measure their average activity levels every second or so. Thus far we can roughly identify the human brain's structural connections. Luckily, scientists and engineers have taken steps to deliver ever clearer data that will enable a deeper look into perhaps the most complex network in the known universe: your brain.

About the Authors

Max Bertolero is director of research and development at Turing Medical in St. Louis, Mo. He received a doctorate in systems neuroscience from the University of California, Berkeley, and undergraduate degrees in philosophy and psychology from Columbia University.

Dani S. Bassett is J. Peter Skirkanich Professor of Bioengineering at the University of Pennsylvania. Their lab studies networks in physical, biological and social systems. In 2014 Bassett became a MacArthur Fellow.

Section 5: Non-Human Brains

5.1   What Makes Our Brains Special?
      By Diana Kwon

5.2   Bird Brains Have as Many Neurons as Some Primates
      By Sara Chodosh

5.3   The Genius of Pinheads: When Little Brains Rule
      By Erik Vance

5.4   Cetaceans' Big Brains Are Linked to Their Rich Social Life
      By Amanda Montañez and Diana Kwon

What Makes Our Brains Special?

By Diana Kwon

The human brain is unique: Our remarkable cognitive capacity has allowed us to invent the wheel, build the pyramids and land on the moon. In fact, scientists sometimes refer to the human brain as the "crowning achievement of evolution."

But what, exactly, makes our brains so special? Some leading arguments have been that our brains have more neurons and expend more energy than would be expected for our size, and that our cerebral cortex, which is responsible for higher cognition, is disproportionately large—accounting for over 80 percent of our total brain mass.

Suzana Herculano-Houzel, a neuroscientist at the Institute of Biomedical Science in Rio de Janeiro, debunked these well-established beliefs in recent years when she discovered a novel way of counting neurons—dissolving brains into a homogenous mixture, or "brain soup." Using this technique she found the number of neurons relative to brain size to be consistent with other primates, and that the cerebral cortex, the region responsible for higher cognition, only holds around 20 percent of all our brain's neurons, a similar proportion found in other mammals. In light of these findings, she argues that the human brain is actually just a linearly scaled-up primate brain that grew in size as we started to consume more calories, thanks to the advent of cooked food.

Other researchers have found that traits once believed to belong solely to humans also exist in other members of the animal kingdom. Monkeys have a sense of fairness. Chimps engage in war. Rats show altruism and exhibit empathy. In a study published last week in *Nature Communications*, neuroscientist Christopher Petkov and his group at Newcastle University found that macaques and humans share brain areas responsible for processing the basic structures of language. [*Scientific American* is part of Nature Publishing Group.]

Although some of the previously proposed reasons our brains are special may have been debunked, there are still many ways in which we are different. They lie in our genes and our ability to adapt to our surroundings. Two other recently published studies add new insight to the debate.

Unique Genetic Signatures

At the genetic level, humans are similar to other animals. We share more than 90 percent of our DNA with our closest relatives, including chimpanzees, bonobos and gorillas. Mice and humans also share many of the same genes—which is why scientists use them as a model to study many human diseases. Studies in recent years, however, have revealed that the way in which genes, the segments of DNA that code for specific proteins, are expressed can be quite different among humans and other animals.

One reason scientists can now unravel these more nuanced differences between the human brain and those of other species is the rise of more robust data collection techniques. For example, scientists at the Allen Institute for Brain Science have developed detailed atlases of the expression patterns of thousands of genes in various species, including those of adult mice and human brains. In a study published last week in *Nature Neuroscience* researchers used these enormous data sets to look for the patterns of gene expression that are shared within the human population. They were able to identify 32 unique signatures within 20,000 genes that appear to be shared across 132 brain regions in six individuals (see a map here). This unique genetic code may help explain what gives rise to our distinctly human traits.

When the researchers compared humans with mice, they found that whereas the genes associated with neurons were well preserved among species, those associated with glial cells—nonneuronal cells with a wide variety of functions—were not. They also found the gene patterns associated with glia overlap with those implicated with disorders of the brain, such as Alzheimer's disease. This adds to the recent developments revealing that glial cells, which for a long time were thought to simply be the brain's support cells, are actually a major player in both development and disease. "It affirms the importance of these glial patterns in brain disease," says Michael Hawrylycz, a computational biologist at the Allen Institute and first author of the study.

This finding may have another important implication—the capacity for plasticity; researchers have found the glia play an important role in shaping the brain. "One interesting thing in the context of [the uniqueness of the human brain] is that you could imagine that one way to enhance the system would be to make it more plastic—I'm hypothesizing here, but [glia] could potentially be one route to do that," says Allen neuroscientist Ed Lein, senior author of the paper. "[But] we still need to do the analysis to see whether this is specific to humans or is common among primates."

From Monkey to Human

Plasticity may be what underlies the specific differences in our brain that lead to our unique cognitive abilities. A study published last week in *Proceedings of the National Academy of Sciences* revealed that human brains may be less genetically inheritable, and therefore more plastic, than those of chimpanzees, our closest ancestors.

Aida Gómez-Robles, an anthropologist at the George Washington University, and her colleagues compared the effect of genes on brain size and organization in 218 human and 206 chimpanzee brains. They found that although brain size was highly heritable in both species, the organization of the cerebral cortex—especially in areas involved in higher-order cognition functions—was much less genetically controlled in humans than in chimps. One potential explanation for this difference, according to the researchers, is that because our brains are less developed than those of our primate cousins at birth, it creates a longer period during which we can be molded by our surroundings.

More research, however, is required to pinpoint exactly where those differences lie. "There are still many things we don't know about what humans share with great apes and with other mammals," Gómez-Robles says. Understanding where we are unique and where we are not will not only shed light on how we became the dominant species on the planet but can also help us better understand ourselves. Knowing where the parallels between humans and other species lie can also help scientists develop more effective therapies and treatments for disorders and diseases.

About the Author

Diana Kwon is a freelance journalist who covers health and the life sciences. She is based in Berlin.

Bird Brains Have as Many Neurons as Some Primates

By Sara Chodosh

I f you own a parrot, you may owe it an apology. "Bird-brained" isn't an insult: although a bird's brain may seem diminutive, its small size only makes its mental capacities more impressive.

Scientists have known for some time that birds are capable of complex cognition—as tool-making crows and discriminating pigeons reveal. The question was how nature had gotten all that neural hardwiring into such a small package. Research published this month in the *Proceedings of the National Academy of Sciences* offers a new explanation: bird brains pack neurons more densely than those of other animals.

For a long time, the prevailing idea was that brain size most directly determined an animal's intelligence and that neuron density didn't vary much across species. In the last 10 to 20 years that perception has changed, especially in mammalian brains where differences in neuronal density have been observed. Bird brains are so small that they clearly require some structural difference to allow them to carry out complex cognition in a compact space, but until now it wasn't clear precisely how they differed.

The new study comes out of an international collaboration between universities in Prague, Vienna, Rio de Janeiro and Sao Paulo, and is the first to quantify the neurons in the avian brain. To do so, the researchers took samples from 28 different species and dissected them into anatomical sections. They then made homogeneous suspensions from each section, stained the nuclei, and divided each into tiny individual samples of suspended cells. These smaller samples each contain approximately the same number of cells, making it relatively easy to quickly and accurately count neurons. Using this method, an entire avian brain can be processed in one day in contrast to the old fashioned approach, which was much more labor- and time-intensive.

(Historically, neuroanatomists had to cut very thin sections of the brain, staining them to show individual cells and counting every cell by hand. Across an entire brain, this method required a huge amount of time and had a high risk for human error.)

Although many in the field expected the bird brain could be densely packed, the extent came as a surprise to the study authors. "My expectation was simply that bird brains should be different from mammals in size and number of neurons," says neuroscientist Suzana Herculano-Houzel, now at Vanderbilt University, one of the senior authors on the paper. "But we didn't have any idea that the difference would be so extreme that in a parrot brain you would have as many neurons as in a mid-size primate."

Previous research on bird intelligence in songbirds and parrots—birds with impressive vocal capabilities—has shown that there are particular pathways in bird brains that enable this complex cognition. But these pathways are made up of millions of neurons, which seemed impossible for such small brains to accomodate. "[It seemed like] there must be something that's lost to make space for this pathway," says neurobiologist Erich Jarvis at the Howard Hughes Medical Institute, who studies these neural pathways and did not participate in the new research. "This paper gives me an explanation: these birds didn't lose neurons for another trait, they just packed things into a tighter space."

For the Birds?

The findings by Herculano-Houzel and her colleagues are just part of a larger effort to better understand bird brain anatomy and intelligence. Until the mid-twentieth century many scientists held the bias that birds were incapable of advanced cognition.

In fact, even the names given to bird neuroanatomy signal their perceived simplicity. A century ago, neurobiologist Ludwig Edinger compared the neuroanatomies of various animals so that he could assemble a more cohesive view of how their brains evolved. But Edinger's understanding of evolution wasn't accurate; he believed that evolution happened linearly in time and space. He thought that primitive areas of the brain must be at one edge of the brain and over time the more complex parts developed in layers on top of each other.

Bird brains have a very different structure from most other intelligent animals, which led Edinger to think that they must not be as smart as mammals. So when he went about naming bird brain structures, he gave them names like "paleostriatum" meaning "old striatum," referring to a fairly primitive area involved in instinctual behaviors and basic motor coordination. He assumed that the brain had evolved from the striatum. But in fact, we now know it evolved from the pallium, an area that carries out reasoning and planning.

In 2005 an international group of experts argued in *Nature Reviews Neuroscience* that the derogatory nomenclature was hindering scientific advances because it inaccurately reflected the brain's sophistication. Their plea ultimately led to new terminology for use in the research community. This change reflects a modern, nuanced view of bird evolution to which Herculano-Houzel hopes her work contributes. She and her colleagues chose to study a variety of species so that they could "get a glimpse into evolution," she explains. "The idea is that if you understand what changes and what doesn't change between modern species, then you could do the detective work to figure out what the first bird brains were made of."

There's still work to be done to prove that these densely packed neurons are directly impacting intelligence, says Jarvis. Nonetheless, he finds the new work impressive: "I hesitate to use the word breakthrough, but I think it's a conceptual breakthrough."

About the Author

Sara Chodosh is a science journalist and former editorial intern for Scientific American Mind *who writes frequently about neuroscience. Her work has also been featured in* Undark *and the* Atlantic.

The Genius of Pinheads: When Little Brains Rule

By Erik Vance

The Samoan moss spider, the world's smallest arachnid at a third of a millimeter, is nearly invisible to the human eye. The largest spider in the world is the goliath bird eater tarantula, which weighs 142 grams and is about the size of a dinner plate. For reference, that is about the same difference in scale between that same tarantula and a bottlenose dolphin.

And yet the bigger spider does not act in more complex ways than its tiny counterpart. "Insects and spiders and the like—in terms of absolute size—have among the tiniest brains we've come across," says William Wcislo, a scientist at the Smithsonian Tropical Research Institute in Panama City. "But their behavior, as far as we can see, is as sophisticated as things that have relatively large brains. So then there's the question: How do they do that?"

No one would argue that a tarantula is as smart as a dolphin or that having a really big brain is not an excellent way to perform complicated tasks. But a growing number of scientists are asking whether it is the only way. Do you need a big brain to hunt elusive prey, design complicated structures or produce complex social dynamics?

For generations scientists have wondered how intelligent creatures developed large brains to perform complicated tasks. But Wcislo is part of a small community of scientists less interested in how brains have grown than how they have shrunk and yet shockingly still perform tasks as well as or better than similar species much larger in size. In other words, it is what scientists call brain miniaturization, not unlike the scaling down in size of the transistors in a computer chip. This research, in fact, may hold clues to innovative design strategies that engineers might incorporate in future generations of computers.

Scientists interested in brain miniaturization often refer to something called Haller's rule, proposed by German neuroscientist

Bernhard Rensch and named for the 18th-century father of physiology, Albrecht von Haller. It holds that smaller creatures will have smaller brains but that the ratio of brain to body size will actually go up. And what is amazing is that few if any creatures on earth violate this rule. "It's extremely general, and it's been known for a long time. And there seem to be no good ideas as to why in the world it's true," says William Eberhard, a spider researcher and frequent collaborator with Wcislo, who also works at the Tropical Research Institute.

Imagine packing for a trip with a massive suitcase and then learning that the plane will accept only luggage half that size. The trip is the same, but the space just got tight, so you will have to be more efficient, and your bag might be bursting at the seams. The same thing happens to some of Eberhard's smaller spiders. "Their brains were not staying in the right parts of their body. In the tiny ones they were going into the legs, and the sternum was bulging out, and it was full of brain. Their bodies were being deformed by these brains," he says.

The comparison of scale in this spider world boggles the mind. Take Eberhard's favorite group of creatures, orb weaver spiders. The largest he has worked with weighs around three grams, whereas the smallest weighs 0.005 milligram—roughly 600,000 times as small as its cousin. For perspective, imagine a normal adult man standing next to a giant who stood 400 kilometers tall and weighed more than 300 blue whales. The giant's brain alone would weigh 910,000 kilograms.

So would such a giant be more intelligent than a human? If the scaling principles hold from the world of spiders, the answer is no, as can be seen by looking closely at the webs they spin.

As a spider constructs a web, it must continually make decisions, finding the most efficient places to attach each thread. And although they are exceptional architects, they do make mistakes—and those mistakes are pretty consistent over time. So Eberhard used these web-making mistakes as a proxy for cognitive capacity. Knowing the incredible costs of having a tiny body and thus an outsize brain, he expected to see that cost reflected in their webs. The smaller spiders should make more mistakes.

Shockingly, they do not. In fact, species to species and even within the species, the number of mistakes was exactly the same. Then a student of Eberhard's tested the little critters, forcing them to build in a constrained environment—inside a piece of tubing about the diameter of a large air-rifle BB. Again, the spiders made the same number of miscalculations, even as newly born nymphs. The same seems to be true for parasitic wasps, which span from the massive tarantula hawk to a fairy wasp that is smaller than a single-celled paramecium. The latter have truly minuscule brains but are equally as adept at locating and ambushing prey. "We haven't yet found any behavioral costs of having a totally tiny brain," Wcislo says.

How could such a tiny brain perform as well as a bigger one? Through vicious, cutthroat evolutionary efficiency. Some tiny creatures actually have shrunken brain cells with dramatically shorter connecting axons, the wirelike extensions from neurons. But even then, there is a lower limit—a cell cannot get smaller than its nucleus (although some beetles may simply jettison the nucleus altogether). And if axons get too short, they start interfering with one another like tangled electrical cabling.

So having a halfway-decent brain is a tough job for small invertebrates. What does this mean for us larger creatures? It turns out that Haller's rule does not care if you are a spider, wasp, bird or even a human. As animals evolve to become smaller because of a change in climate or other selective pressures, their brain demands an ever higher percentage of energy and real estate in their body.

One species of salamander that, like insects, can vary wildly in size has evolved a thinner skull to make room for its brain. And although it is not yet clear how all this applies to humans, we do know that human brains have shrunk over the past 10,000 years. Perhaps rather than becoming less intelligent, our ancestors' brains were just becoming more efficient.

Diego Ocampo, a biologist currently finishing his Ph.D. at the University of Miami, took a survey of more than 70 bird species and found that they perfectly follow Haller's rule, with the smallest ones having proportionally larger brains. But when he looked at individual groups, he noticed hummingbirds had their own supercharged version of the rule. Take two species of hummingbird. The violet sabrewing, a sizable bird at 12 grams, is about 2.4 percent brain. Meanwhile the striped-throated hermit, which is a fifth the size, is 4.8 percent brain. Compared with other creatures, these numbers are oddly low. Far bigger birds that he sampled, such as thornbills, have a brain that takes up an ungainly 7 percent of their body.

It is as if the hummingbirds as a group have come up with a far more efficient type of brain than other birds—a slight bending of Haller's rule. And if that was not enough, the hermit, far from being a simpleton, actually demonstrates the most complex behaviors. Whereas the sabrewing tends to sit and guard a single plant, the hermit memorizes complex lines to follow through the forest to find food.

What if birds have unlocked some kind of ultraefficient brain design that allows them to do more with less? Certainly this would explain some of the stupendous abilities observed in, say, African grey parrots, which can identify shapes and even count, as well as corvids, which have an equivalent number of neurons to some primates and, it is suggested, may even be self-aware. Do not forget octopuses, which have very primitive brains and yet perform tasks that rival those of dogs.

Lars Chittka, who studies bee behavior and intelligence at Queen Mary University of London, flips these questions about animal smarts on their head. It is not that they require large brains to do complicated things, he says, it is that complicated behavior really does not require much brainpower. "The task that requires a large brain hasn't been discovered yet," he says. "You can do a whole lot with very little brains." Some wasps, he says, are able to recognize the faces of every other wasp in their communities. But when he looks at their brain, there is nothing to explain such an impressive ability. Chittka suggests facial recognition may have evolved from simpler abilities, such as recognizing food sources. And given that bees have complex social interactions, symbolic language and excellent spatial memory, there is not really much to separate their intelligence from that of, say, a rodent.

Still, it stretches credibility to compare two species from vastly different parts of the animal kingdom and even harder to understand how physiology corresponds to specific behaviors. But, Eberhard says, any animal that has been pushed "up against the wall of Haller's rule" by evolving to a smaller size while maintaining complicated behaviors is bound to have come up with a few interesting ways to streamline its brain.

Wcislo compares large animals such as whales and perhaps humans, with the large Apple IIe computers that sat on so many desks in the 1980s and revolutionized personal computing. They were powerful tools, but there was lots of wasted space and excess heat production. Now compare that with modern iPhones, and you see the power of miniaturization.

So maybe it is not surprising that Wcislo's work has attracted the attention of Silicon Valley. His oldest and most devoted funder is Frank Levinson, a venture capitalist and founder of the fiber-optics giant Finisar. To explain why he started investing in bug research, Levinson describes the time he watched a pair of male butterflies near his home compete for a female's attention, ducking and weaving around a bush. "The best chip out of Intel can't fly, can't dance, can't romance a woman, can't dogfight," he says. "I don't know anything in silicon that could do anything remotely as complex as this."

If tiny animals have learned to do more with less, what is stopping electronics from doing the same?

Levinson says electronics companies today are obsessed with artificial intelligence—how to make machines more humanlike—at the same time that the increase in computing speeds seem to be slowing down for the first time since the 1970s. So, Levinson says, there is a huge need to both understand how intelligence works and make circuits smaller and more efficient. In other words, more insectlike.

Insects provide plenty of examples of high-performing computational machines. Take Wcislo's latest obsession, nocturnal sweat bees that live under a jungle canopy with 10 to 20 times less light than on a moonless night. It is so dark that the laws of physics say there are not enough photons to distinguish a visual signal from background noise. "How the hell do they see?" Wcislo says. "They should not be able to see." It seems their tiny brain acts as a filter for the image, like night-vision goggles, extracting an image out of the surrounding darkness. He is also training ants to walk through mazes and then comparing their brain with those of other ants living less intellectually challenging lives. These are the kinds of questions that may suggest cutting-edge materials and designs to allow computers to shrink as fast as animal brains have.

At the end of the day, insect brains offer more than just incredible efficiency—they also offer simplicity. Investigations into artificial human intelligence are tricky, partly because the human brain is inordinately complex. But as these scientists are finding, there is much you can do with a very small, efficient brain. Perhaps there is more programmers can learn from them as well.

"Silicon Valley is always looking for those new niches," Levinson says. "One interesting place to look is with [Wcislo] and the guys studying something as simple as ants and bees and spiders—and see what they can tell us about thought processes and learning."

About the Author

Erik Vance is a science writer and relatively new father. His first book, Suggestible You *(National Geographic, 2016), is about how belief affects the brain.*

Cetaceans' Big Brains Are Linked to Their Rich Social Life

By Amanda Montañez and Diana Kwon

K iller whales have group-specific dialects, sperm whales babysit one another's young and bottlenose dolphins cooperate with other species. These social skills are all closely linked with the aquatic mammals' brain sizes, according to a recent study in *Nature Ecology & Evolution*.

Scientists first proposed a relation between social living and brain expansion, or encephalization, nearly three decades ago, when they observed that primate species with larger brains typically lived in bigger groups. This theory was later broadened to associate brain size with other social characteristics, such as resolving conflicts and allocating food.

Michael Muthukrishna, an economic psychologist at the London School of Economics, and his colleagues went searching for a similar link between big brains and sociality in cetaceans—the mammalian order that includes whales, dolphins and porpoises. They compiled a comprehensive data set of cetacean brain and body mass, group size and social characteristics. The team's analyses, which covered 90 species, revealed that brain size was best predicted by a score based on various social behaviors such as cooperation with other species, group hunting and complex vocalizations. Bigger brains were also linked to other factors, including dietary richness and geographical range.

The authors say these results are consistent with theories that cetaceans developed large brains to deal with the challenges of living in information-rich social environments. Yet Robert Barton, an evolutionary biologist at Durham University in England, who did not take part in the work, cautions against drawing conclusions about causation from correlation. He also asserts that it is important to examine specific regions of the brain because they might evolve differently. For example, his own research team has found that nocturnal primates' brains develop larger olfactory structures—regions associated with smell—than those found in species active during the day.

Muthukrishna notes that his study's main limitation is the lack of available research on many cetacean species. Discovering more about whales and dolphins could reveal that other factors—such as life span and the duration of the juvenile phase—might also be involved in brain size, he adds.

Understanding how cetaceans developed such big brains could ultimately help us piece together humanity's own evolutionary history. Because these animals occupy a completely different environment than people do, Muthukrishna says, "they provide us with a useful control group for testing hypotheses about human evolution."

About the Authors

Amanda Montañez has been a graphics editor at Scientific American since 2015. She produces and art directs information graphics for the Scientific American website and print magazine. Amanda has a bachelor's degree in studio art from Smith College and a master's in biomedical communications from the University of Toronto. Before starting in journalism, she worked as a freelance medical illustrator.

Diana Kwon is a freelance journalist who covers health and the life sciences. She is based in Berlin.

Section 6: Treating the Brain

6.1 Five Types of Research, Underexplored until Recently, Could Produce Alzheimer's Treatments
By Kenneth S. Kosik

6.2 New Research Points to Causes for Brain Disorders with No Obvious Injury
By Z Paige L'Erario

6.3 Forgotten Memories of Traumatic Events Get Some Backing from Brain-Imaging Studies
By Joshua Kendall

6.4 The Invisible Victims of Traumatic Brain Injury
By Anne P. DePrince and Kim Gorgens

6.5 Elon Musk's Secretive Brain Tech Company Debuts a Sophisticated Neural Implant
By Tanya Lewis and Gary Stix

6.6 New Brain Implant Turns Visualized Letters into Text
By Bret Stetka

Five Types of Research, Underexplored until Recently, Could Produce Alzheimer's Treatments

By Kenneth S. Kosik

No fundamental obstacle prevents us from developing an effective treatment for Alzheimer's disease. Other troubles of human nature, such as violence, greed and intolerance, have a bewildering variety of daunting causes and uncertainties. But Alzheimer's, at its core, is a problem of cell biology whose solution should be well within our reach. There is a fairly good chance that the scientific community might already have an unrecognized treatment stored away in a laboratory freezer among numerous vials of chemicals. And major insights may now reside, waiting to be noticed, in big databases or registries of clinical records, neuropsychological profiles, brain-imaging studies, biological markers in blood and spinal fluid, genomes, protein analyses, neuron recordings, or animal and cell culture models.

But we have missed those clues because for decades we have spent too much time chasing every glossy new finding in Alzheimer's research and too little time thinking deeply about the underlying biology of this ailment. Instead our work has been driven by a number of assumptions. Among those assumptions has been the central and dominant role of the protein fragment called beta-amyloid. A large amount of data supports the idea that beta-amyloid plays an important part in the disease. We have developed drugs that can reduce concentrations of the protein fragments in people with Alzheimer's, yet by and large they have not stopped patients' cognitive decline in any meaningful way.

It now seems simplistic to conclude that eliminating or inhibiting beta-amyloid will cure or treat those suffering from the disease, especially without far deeper and more comprehensive knowledge of how it develops and progresses. We have not been barking up a completely wrong research tree, but our zeal has led us to ignore other trees and even the roots of this particular one.

It is time to go back to basics. I have been a scientist involved in Alzheimer's research for three decades, part of large projects investigating families with a high risk of Alzheimer's, prevention strategies and the physiology of damage to brain cells that is part of the illness. I and my colleagues, who work across many scientific and medical disciplines, believe that we need to reexamine the fundamental physiology and biology of Alzheimer's, as well as reassess the contents of databases and our lab refrigerators for clues that we may have overlooked. This approach will let us develop theories and models of the way this illness progresses, and we can use those ideas to derive novel strategies to combat the disease.

There are at least five potentially fruitful and timely research directions—areas based on important discoveries made in the past several years—that can extend our knowledge, and I believe that they are quite likely to yield insights needed to find effective treatments. These areas range from malfunctions in the way brain cells get rid of problem proteins, to damage caused by inflammation, to trouble with the ways that cells send electrical signals to one another. These are different domains, but in a person they overlap to create illness in the brain, and individually or in tandem they may lie behind the terrible damage done by Alzheimer's.

Protein-Disposal Problems

Beginning in the early 1900s, several neuropathologists—including Alois Alzheimer, the scientist after whom the disease is named—described microscopic lesions in the brains of patients who had died with various forms of dementia. Today we know these are clumps of misshapen proteins. In the case of Alzheimer's, some of the clumps consist of pieces of beta-amyloid protein. They sit between neurons and are called senile plaques. Other clumps reside within neurons, made of a protein known as tau, and are called neurofibrillary tangles.

What we still do not know, more than a century later, is why cells fail to remove these abnormal lumps. Cellular mechanisms for the removal of damaged proteins are as ancient as life itself. What has gone wrong in the case of Alzheimer's? This question is as central to the disease process as a loss of control over cell proliferation is to the progression of cancer. Some recent observations from researchers at the Washington University at St. Louis, among other institutions, indicate that abnormal proteins may find their way out of cells, perhaps evading their natural detection systems for bad molecules. We do not know how they do so, but figuring it out might be a very useful way to start a new search for how and why Alzheimer's progresses.

Cells have two major systems for the removal of abnormal proteins: the ubiquitin-proteasome system (UPS) and autophagy. In the former, proteins are inserted into a barrel-shaped cell structure called the proteasome, where they are chewed up into reusable parts; in the latter, the cell wraps up aberrant proteins and totally destroys them. In neurons, these systems are co-opted to control the composition of cell-signaling connections—formed by anatomical structures known as axons, dendrites and synapses—as they are strengthened or weakened during learning. (Sometimes neurons extrude damaged proteins and turn over their destruction to microglia, brain cells that are part of the immune system.)

The decision about whether to shuttle an abnormal protein toward the UPS or autophagy is mainly based on the protein's size. The proteasome has a narrow, pore-like opening at each end that can accept a small, fine, threadlike protein strand. Inside it are enzymes that break the protein down into its constituent amino acids, which are recycled for use in the synthesis of new proteins. Larger molecules that do not fit into the proteasome, such as protein clumps and old, misshapen proteins with age-related damage, get shuttled toward the autophagy system and its more powerful engine of destruction, the lysosome.

In Alzheimer's, something goes wrong and leaves brain cells with these chunks of tau and amyloid that further damage or choke them. So we could learn an enormous amount about the pathology of Alzheimer's if we understood the details of these systems. We need to examine specific differences in the degradation pathways in different subtypes of neurons, as well as the precise mechanism by which these disposal systems recognize abnormal proteins. Malformations in proteins such as tau do not happen in a single step. Proteins may harbor mutations and accumulate modifications that predispose them to misfolding, which can be followed by aggregation into larger and larger structures in a multistage process. As proteins progress along this pathway, at what point do surveillance systems kick in and recognize them as abnormal? In-depth knowledge about these kinds of processes could lead us to a more strategic approach to treatment and intervention with drugs.

One intriguing finding that plays into our understanding of such evasion is that tau can travel out of cells and into the spaces between them, and from there it gets taken up by neighboring cells. What purpose this transit system serves is unknown. Is exchange of the protein among cells normal, or do cells disgorge abnormal tau to rid themselves of a toxic substance? We think that in Alzheimer's, at least some of the tau protein outside cells is already misfolded. We believe this because when such tau enters a neighboring cell, it forms a template, an abnormal pattern, that other tau proteins in that cell use to shape themselves in similar odd ways. When it spreads, tau in neighboring cells copies the specific shape of the entering tau protein.

The observations of tau outside cells have prompted some to speculate that the protein could be intercepted and cleared at that point by an antibody delivered to the patient. But that approach is unlikely to work unless we know exactly how tau is misshapen when it does its damage. This precise structure is necessary information for designing a highly specific antibody. Another open question is where tau resides in the complex space between cells. More specifically, does it move across synapses, where two neurons transmit their signals? This synaptic cleft is a narrow gap that is not easily accessible to an antibody. Potentially more promising approaches are to understand exactly how tau is extruded from cells and the receptors that neighboring cells use to pick the protein up; recent experiments in my lab may point to the identity of one such receptor.

Identifying Protein Changes

One major recent advance in Alzheimer's research was the imaging of abnormal tau within a cell, snarled in a neurofibrillary tangle, at a level of detail never before seen. This remarkable image, published in 2017 in *Nature*, showed thousands of tau proteins aligned as pairs tightly locked in a C-shape configuration. It is possible that features seen in this solid inclusion could provide the information necessary to design small molecules that fit within the crevices of the abnormal protein and pull it apart to disrupt the disease process.

But breaking up these structures is a challenging goal for many reasons, not the least of which is how strongly the whole tangle is held together. A more successful direction could be to determine the sequence of microscopic events that takes these tau proteins from their typical liquidlike state to the more rigid and solid state seen in that image and to discover the protein modifications that predispose tau toward this change.

The switch from liquid to solid is called a phase transition. Biologists' interest in such transitions in living cells is now surging because of their possible role in disease. Physical chemists have studied phase separation, such as the condensation of oil drops in water, for many years. Oil and water are both liquids, yet they remain separated because of a balance of attractive and repellent forces. The advantage of phase separation for living cells is that it concentrates a specific set of molecules in one place, which aids certain cellular activities. Multiple proteins near a gene, for instance, can condense to control the expression of that gene, as shown in a 2018 paper in *Science*. Such a condensed set of proteins, though still in a liquid state, do not diffuse away; they are held together as a droplet by weak physical forces. This configuration allows sets of proteins to move and work together without being wrapped together in a membrane, which would require resource-costly maintenance from the cell.

Some proteins, such as tau, are tightly packed when they are located within a droplet, and the high concentrations could make them prone to aggregation into a tangle. Proteins that form droplets in this way share a property known as intrinsic disorder. Like the Greek god Proteus, they can assume numerous shapes, in contrast to more ordered proteins that are limited to a few specific forms. Different shapes require different energy levels. At times, some intrinsically disordered proteins fold into such a low energy state that they cannot shift out of it, which essentially increases their rigidity. And that may exacerbate their tendency to tangle together.

Cells also pack proteins and other molecules prone to phase transitions in membraneless organelles called stress granules and RNA granules. When certain proteins and RNAs coalesce in such granules, they pack tightly together but typically remain in a liquid state. At a certain density, however, they may become predisposed to more clumping and to a phase change to a solid, a change that would increase their ability to cause brain damage and would make them harder for cell-disposal systems to remove. That is why we need to better understand the conditions that trigger this process.

The Influence of Genes

In middle-aged people, Alzheimer's can arise from genetic mutations in three genes (*APP, PSEN1* and *PSEN2*) that cause a rare familial form of the disease, a frightful inheritance passed from one generation to the next. But the vast majority of the time, Alzheimer's shows up in individuals older than 65 and does not involve these genes. By combing through tens of thousands of genomes, geneticists have now discovered other DNA changes, about two dozen gene variants, that do increase risk by a small amount. The most influential of these alternative forms is a version of the gene *APOE* known as the e4 variant. A combination of several risk-gene variants adds to one's likelihood of getting the disease. (Because gene variants are frequently associated with ethnicity, we need a much more inclusive data set than the mostly Caucasian-based gene analyses and registries currently available to make a reliable assessment of genetic risk in all populations.)

Each of these variants opens a different door through which we can explore the ways that a small change in our genomes can heighten our likelihood of acquiring Alzheimer's. Some of the more frequently seen variants, and thus the most interesting doors, are genes or other stretches of DNA in the microglia. In a 2019 *Science* paper examining these immune system cells, scientists found one variant associated with Alzheimer's risk in a gene known as *BIN1*. This gene is normally involved in the way microglia engulf potentially harmful outside molecules and move them into the cell, protecting nearby neurons. The variant can affect how efficiently microglia clean up stray proteins.

In microglia and other cells, certain gene variants are also associated with age and sex. Differences exist between men and women, for example, for genes on the 22 pairs of non-sex chromosomes and for genes expressed on the X and Y chromosomes. The effects of these variants may have something to do with the higher rates of Alzheimer's in women, which hold even with correction for women's longer life spans. Overall the small effects of any single gene variant associated with Alzheimer's probably contribute, each in its own limited way, to individual differences in the way we handle amyloid and tau accumulations. We need to nail down the how and why of these contributions.

Taming Inflammation

When the brain detects a source of damage such as amyloid plaques or tau neurofibrillary tangles, it sounds an alert and releases a barrage of immune system molecules called cytokines, along with a variety of attack cells. This response stems from the microglia, in large part, and it causes an inflammatory reaction intended to destroy any tissue harboring the trouble spots. This brutelike "innate" system operates quite differently from the more refined "adaptive" immune system, which generates immune cells and antibodies that react only to specific invaders, such as bacteria or viruses, and that mount a narrower, more precise defense. The broader innate response dominates in Alzheimer's. As the lesions proliferate beyond the ability of a neuron's internal machinery to get rid of detritus, this general inflammatory response kicks in and, unfortunately, often hits still healthy cells in the brain. Scientists at the University of California, Irvine, recently have found that eliminating the aged microglia in older mice prompted the animals to repopulate their brains with fresh microglia. This rejuvenation improved spatial memory, reversed age-related changes in neuronal gene expression, and increased the birth of new neurons, as well as the density of their dendrites.

This assault triggered by amyloid and tau probably happens on top of a low level of inflammation in the brain that occurs naturally with aging. Many older people have increased concentrations of proinflammatory cytokines such as tumor necrosis factor (TNF), suggesting that a slight inflammatory state exists throughout the body at this point in life. Aging is highly variable among humans, and the differences mean the progress and the effects of Alzheimer's are quite variable as well. Some of this diversity can probably be attributed to individual variation in human immune systems. Different people inherit distinct configurations of genes involved in immune responses. In addition, during our lives our systems are shaped by nonheritable influences. We get different exposures to symbiotic microbes in places such as our gut and to pathogenic microbes from our surroundings. This all suggests that exposure of the immune system to various pathogens, as well as our genetic differences, may contribute to the way Alzheimer's develops by establishing an individual immune profile, or "immunotype."

The challenge for researchers who want to stop the brain damage caused by widespread inflammation is to distinguish the desirable immune responses the brain uses to combat developing problems and ordinary age-induced degradation from the other, more reckless immune responses to the advancing pathology of Alzheimer's. The research community would like to tame brain inflammation caused by the disease but does not yet know how to deliver an intervention with precision.

Electrical Disconnections

The brain is an electrical organ: its most defining feature is its ability to encode and convey information in the form of electrical signals passed between neurons, usually by chemicals called neurotransmitters. How Alzheimer's impairs brain cells' signaling and disrupts the way they assemble into functional memory circuits has been insufficiently studied. But now the ability to detect both structural and functional connections is burgeoning thanks to technical advances that allow us to visualize these links in exquisite detail.

Some of these advances involve optogenetics, a way for scientists to stimulate specific neurons in an animal's brain using light. Researchers can offer the animal a reward or fearful experience, then detect which genes become more active. This approach, in an impressive achievement, is now allowing researchers to observe and manipulate specific neurons that encode a specific memory known as an engram, as noted in a 2020 paper in *Science*. When those cells were stimulated by light alone after the initial experience, the memory of it was recalled. If we can figure out the biology that drives the formation of these electrical memory connections, that information will be crucial in helping us understand how Alzheimer's pathology interrupts this neural circuitry.

Neuroscientists made another advance this year when they discovered that microglia seem to be involved in making the brain forget these engrams by eliminating the synapses that normally connect neurons.

We also know that neurotransmitters are affected in different ways by some of the proteins involved in Alzheimer's pathology. Tau, for instance, accumulates in neurons that use the neurotransmitter glutamate and work to excite signals. But other neurons that inhibit signals—signaling relies on good start-and-stop mechanisms—release a different neurotransmitter, GABA, and are less affected by tau accumulation. The basis for this cellular selectivity and its consequences is unknown, and we need to understand it much better.

Scientists have also seen that neuronal activity enhances tau's spread, which could be another important part of the Alzheimer's puzzle.

Not only are signaling cell types affected differently by the disease process, but effects vary in different brain areas, too. For example, areas of the brain related to memory, emotions and sleep are severely damaged, whereas centers related to primary motor and sensory function are relatively spared. One study found that regions of the brain activated when our minds wander, the so-called default or resting state, are the same places where amyloid plaques are first deposited. But we must be cautious in drawing conclusions—a wandering mind does not necessarily cause amyloid deposition.

Sleep is another electrical state of the brain that is increasingly recognized as a factor in the development of Alzheimer's. Levels of both amyloid and tau fluctuate during the normal sleep-wake cycle, and sleep deprivation acutely increases the production of amyloid and decreases its clearance. Deep sleep evokes rhythmic waves of cerebrospinal fluid that may serve to clear toxins, including amyloid, from the brain. Unfortunately, this kind of sleep diminishes with aging. This observation could stimulate work on pharmacological approaches designed to specifically restore deep sleep.

Shared Ideas

These research areas are not the be-all and end-all of a rejuvenated Alzheimer's science agenda. There are certainly more. But these five avenues are intertwined and, like biology itself, can be investigated in many cross-fertilizing ways. One hope I have is that as basic science fills in missing information—particularly quantitative information—computational modelers and theoreticians will step in to help predict the impact of Alzheimer's pathology on brain circuitry and cellular pathways. I also would like to see these research directions prompt investigators to think collectively and systematically and to share their ideas in constructive ways. This is how we can come together to push back our ignorance about this terrible disease.

Referenced

Proinflammatory Cytokines, Aging, and Age-Related Diseases. M. Michaud et al. in *Journal of the American Medical Directors Association*, Vol. 14, No. 12, pages 877–882; December 2013.

Cryo-EM Structures of Tau Filaments from Alzheimer's Disease. A.W.P. Fitzpatrick et al. in *Nature*, Vol. 547, pages 185–190; July 17, 2017.

Memory Engrams: Recalling the Past and Imagining the Future. Sheena A. Josselyn and Susumu Tonegawa in *Science*, Vol. 367, Article No. eaaw4325; January 2020.

About the Author

Kenneth S. Kosik is a physician-scientist who has led large research projects about early-onset Alzheimer's disease. His laboratory helped to discover the tangles of tau protein in the brain that are important hallmarks of the illness. He is Harriman Professor of Neuroscience Research and co-director of the Neuroscience Research Institute at the University of California, Santa Barbara.

New Research Points to Causes for Brain Disorders with No Obvious Injury

By Z Paige L'Erario

I magine your daughter has lost the ability to walk, and so you take her to the emergency room. How would you feel if you then overheard the doctor who saw your child laughing at her situation with colleagues? This scenario may sound absurd, but it's based on a true story.

In 2021 researchers published several anecdotes from real cases involving functional neurological disorder (FND). What the vignettes reveal is that medical professionals, including nurses, ambulance drivers and physicians, sometimes treat this condition without concern, as though patients were simply faking their behavior. In my own experience as a neurologist, I have overheard doctors dismiss and laugh at their patients' FND symptoms when they are behind closed doors.

Although the disorder is not well known to the public, FND is actually one of the most common conditions that I and other neurologists encounter. In it, abnormal brain functioning causes physical symptoms to appear. FND comes in many forms, with symptoms that can include seizures, inability to move a limb and movement disorders. People may lose consciousness or their ability to move or walk, or they may experience abnormal tremors or tics. The ailment can be highly disabling and just as costly as neurological conditions with structural origins such as amyotrophic lateral sclerosis (also known as Lou Gehrig's disease), multiple sclerosis and Parkinson's disease.

Although men can develop FND, young to middle-aged women receive this diagnosis most frequently. During the first two years of the COVID pandemic, FND briefly made international headlines when vocal and motor tics such as repeating words or clapping uncontrollably spread with social media usage, particularly among adolescent girls.

So why would a medical professional accuse someone who has lost control of their limbs or has experienced a seizure of faking their symptoms? Unfortunately, many such professionals have a poor or outdated understanding of FND, despite the frequency with which they encounter it. Because nothing is structurally wrong with the patient's brain—clinical testing reveals no obvious injury—physicians may write symptoms off as "all in their head" or dismiss them as psychological. That response, recent research shows, can harm a person who is already suffering. Fortunately, there is another path forward, rooted in sensitivity, respect and new evidence-based approaches.

Historically FND was called conversion disorder. The term came from the belief that traumatic stress was "converted" into functional neurological symptoms via psychological mechanisms. We now know that this understanding is incomplete. Stress and trauma can play a part. In fact, some researchers believe the unique global stressors our society faced during the COVID pandemic increased some people's susceptibility to the condition. But not every person with FND has experienced a traumatic event. New research suggests that biological susceptibility and exposure to stressful events over a lifetime may make a person more vulnerable to developing FND. In fact, relatively minor stressful events such as work-related stress, a viral infection or a small physical accident often precede the onset of FND symptoms.

Recent advances in brain imaging indicate that FND is caused by abnormalities in the functioning of brain networks. Some experts use the analogy that the brain's hardware (or structure) is fine, but the software (or processing) is malfunctioning. For example, studies suggest that in FND, several networks of electrical and chemical signaling pathways between groups of neurons or larger brain regions are not working together as typically expected. These networks include structures of the limbic system, such as the amygdala, that are important in our brain's processing of emotions or stress. Among people with FND, the amygdala is more active when subjected to sad or fearful stimuli. Other brain functions involved in FND include how we plan and interpret sensations in response to our movements, as well as our abilities to pay attention, be aware of our body and experience the feeling of control over our person.

Neuroimaging underscores that people with FND are not "faking" anything. Scientists have found decreased activity in supplementary motor areas and the right temporoparietal junction, which influence whether a patient's symptoms feel under their control. There are also abnormalities in the connections between brain areas responsible for interpreting internal physical sensations and motor planning. These differences in brain activity may help explain one key way that FND differs from other disorders that feature tics, such as the structural neurological condition Tourette's syndrome. As a research team at the University of Calgary in Canada explored in a paper published last November, people with Tourette's report some degree of control in suppressing their tics. In contrast, the symptoms of FND feel entirely involuntary.

Clinicians are also finding better ways to diagnose FND. In the past, neurologists considered conversion disorder to be a diagnosis of exclusion, meaning a diagnosis was made after physicians had ruled out structural neurological abnormality through examination, radiological imaging, laboratory studies and neurophysiological testing such as electroencephalography (EEG). As a result, many patients with FND felt their doctor had told them what they didn't have, not what they did have.

But in the past decade neurologists have developed diagnostic criteria to determine which symptoms are linked to functional brain abnormalities. These emphasize characteristic "positive," or "rule-in," findings based on a neurologist's physical examination, which can predict FND as the basis for a patient's symptoms. For example, a FND patient's symptoms may be inconsistent or change when distracted with another task. A combination of a thorough neurological examination, EEG, brain imaging and lab testing can show whether a person's symptoms are consistent with a structural brain pathology—for instance, a stroke or a brain tumor—or a functional condition such as FND.

Together these advances in the diagnosis and understanding of FND mean doctors are in a better position than ever to identify and understand this disorder. Nevertheless, many patients still have the disorienting, distressing experience of being treated with dismissal or disbelief by medical professionals.

This reaction has damaging consequences. In January a collaboration of researchers at the University of Sheffield in England, Arizona State University and the New York–based Northeast Regional Epilepsy Group laid out case studies and other evidence that clinicians' unsupportive responses to their patients may contribute to a sense of shame in people who are already suffering psychologically from their functional symptoms. In fact, being prone to shame may itself be an additional risk factor for FND.

This connection to shame and stigma takes on an even greater weight when we consider that marginalized groups such as members of the LGBTQ+ community may be at increased risk for functional disorders. A person experiencing stressors such as discrimination, bias and stigma because of their identity can internalize feelings of shame when their psychosocial support systems and coping mechanisms are inadequate or overwhelmed. If someone in this situation has FND, receiving treatment from a doctor who lacks empathy or a current understanding of the condition only makes things worse. Telling a patient their condition is "in their head" contributes to medical misinformation and further stigmatizes people with these disorders.

But this problem can be addressed. Researchers have found that how empathetically a doctor informs their patient about an FND diagnosis influences that patient's likelihood of accepting the diagnosis and successfully completing treatment. And appropriate treatment works. Therapy may combine psychoeducation, medication for any coexisting mental health conditions, psychotherapy and physiotherapy. Outcomes for people who receive sensitive and appropriate care are actually very good.

This year my colleagues and I will publish our observations on the treatment of LGBTQ+ people with FND. Our preliminary findings are promising. Most patients had improvement or complete resolution of their functional symptoms after treatment. In some of our patients, these results can be quite important. We have treated people with functional blindness who then regained the ability to see, and we have watched those in wheelchairs regain the ability to walk. In short, care and compassion can be powerful medicine.

This is an opinion and analysis article, and the views expressed by the author or authors are not necessarily those of Scientific American.

About the Author

Z Paige L'Erario is a board-certified neurologist and transgender activist. They are currently a graduate student of social service at Fordham University and vice chair of the LGBTQI Section of the American Academy of Neurology.

Forgotten Memories of Traumatic Events Get Some Backing from Brain-Imaging Studies

By Joshua Kendall

When adults claim to have suddenly recalled painful events from their childhood, are those memories likely to be accurate? This question is the basis of the "memory wars" that have roiled psychology for decades. And the validity of buried trauma turns up as a point of contention in court cases and in television and movie story lines.

Warnings about the reliability of a forgotten traumatic event that is later recalled—known formally as a delayed memory—have been endorsed by leading mental health organizations such as the American Psychiatric Association (APA). The skepticism is based on a body of research showing that memory is unreliable and that simple manipulations in the lab can make people believe they had an experience that never happened. Some prominent cases of recovered memory of child abuse have turned out to be false, elicited by overzealous therapists.

But psychotherapists who specialize in treating adult survivors of childhood trauma argue that laboratory experiments do not rule out the possibility that some delayed memories recalled by adults are factual. Trauma therapists assert that abuse experienced early in life can overwhelm the central nervous system, causing children to split off a painful memory from conscious awareness. They maintain that this psychological defense mechanism—known as dissociative amnesia—turns up routinely in the patients they encounter.

Tensions between the two positions have often been framed as a debate between hard-core scientists on the false-memory side and therapists in clinical practice in the delayed-memory camp. But clinicians who also do research have been publishing peer-reviewed studies of dissociative amnesia in leading journals for decades. A study published in February in the *American Journal of Psychiatry*, the flagship journal of the APA, highlights the considerable scientific evidence that bolsters the arguments of trauma therapists.

The new paper uses magnetic resonance imaging (MRI) to study amnesia, along with various other dissociative experiences that are often said to occur in the wake of severe child abuse, such as feelings of unreality and depersonalization. In an editorial published in the same issue of the journal, Vinod Menon, a professor of psychiatry and behavioral sciences at the Stanford University School of Medicine, praised the researchers for "[uncovering] a potential brain circuit mechanism underlying individual differences in dissociative symptoms in adults with early-life trauma and PTSD [post-traumatic stress disorder]."

Milissa Kaufman is senior author of the new MRI study and head of the dissociative disorders and trauma research program at McLean Hospital, a teaching hospital affiliated with Harvard Medical School. She notes that, as with earlier MRI studies of trauma survivors, this one shows that there is a neurological basis for dissociative symptoms such as amnesia. "We think that these brain studies can help reduce the stigma associated with our work," Kaufman says. "Like many therapists who treat adult survivors of severe child abuse, I have seen some patients who recover memories of abuse."

Since 1980, dissociative amnesia has been listed as a common symptom of PSTD in every edition of the *Diagnostic and Statistical Manual of Mental Disorders* (*DSM*)—psychiatry's diagnostic bible. The condition has been backed up not just by psychiatric case studies but by dozens of studies involving victims of child abuse, natural disaster, torture, rape, kidnapping, wartime violence and other trauma.

For example, two decades ago psychiatrist James Chu, then director of the trauma and dissociative disorders program at McLean Hospital, published a study involving dozens of women receiving in-patient treatment who had experienced childhood abuse. A majority of the women reported previously having partial or complete amnesia of these events, which they typically remembered not in a therapy session but while at home alone or with family or friends. In many instances, Chu wrote, these women "were able to find strong corroboration of their recovered memories."

False-memory proponents have warned that the use of leading questions by investigators might seed an untrue recollection. As psychiatrist Michael I. Goode wrote of Chu's Study in a letter to the editor, "Participants were asked if 'there was a period during which they did not remember that this [traumatic] experience happened.' With this question alone, the actuality of the traumatic experience was inherently validated by the investigators."

MRI studies conducted over the past two decades have found that PTSD patients with dissociative amnesia exhibit reduced activity in the amygdala—a brain region that controls the processing of emotion—and increased activity in the prefrontal cortex, which controls planning, focus and other executive functioning skills. In contrast, PTSD patients who report no lapse in their memories of trauma exhibit increased activity in the amygdala and reduced activity in the prefrontal cortex.

"The reason for these differences in neuronal circuitry is that PTSD patients with dissociative symptoms such as amnesia and depersonalization—a group comprising somewhere between 15 and 30 percent of all PTSD patients—shut down emotionally in response to trauma," says Ruth Lanius, a professor of psychiatry and director of the PTSD research unit at the University of Western Ontario, who has conducted several of these MRI studies. Children may try to detach from abuse to avoid intolerable emotional pain, which can result in forgetting an experience for many years, she maintains. "Dissociation involves a psychological escape when a physical escape is not possible," Lanius adds.

False-memory researchers remain skeptical of the brain-imaging studies. Henry Otgaar, a professor of legal psychology at Maastricht University in the Netherlands, who has co-authored more than 100 academic publications on false-memory research and who often serves as an expert witness for defendants in abuse cases,maintains that intact autobiographical memories are rarely—if ever—repressed.

"These brain studies provide biological evidence just for the *claims* of patients who report memory loss due to dissociation," he says. "There are many alternative explanations for these correlations—say, retrograde amnesia, in which the forgetting is due to a brain injury."

In an effort to provide a firmer grounding for their arguments, Kaufman and her McLean colleagues used artificial intelligence to develop a model of the connections between diverse brain networks that could account for dissociative symptoms. They fed the computer MRI data on 65 women with histories of childhood abuse who had been diagnosed with PTSD, along with their scores on a commonly used inventory of dissociative symptoms. "The computer did the rest," Kaufman says.

Her key finding is that severe dissociative symptoms likely involve the connections between two specific brain networks that are active at the same time: the so-called default mode network—which kicks in when the mind is at rest and involves remembering the past and envisioning the future—and the frontoparietal control network—which is involved in problem-solving.

The McLean study is not the first attempt to apply machine learning to dissociative symptoms. In a paper published in the September 2019 issue of the *British Journal of Psychiatry*, researchers showed how MRI scans of the brain structures of 75 women—32 with dissociative identity disorder, for which dissociative amnesia is a key symptom, and 43 matched controls—could discriminate between people with or without the disorder nearly 75 percent of the time.

Kaufman says additional research needs to be carried out before clinicians can begin using brain connectivity as a diagnostic tool to assess the severity of dissociative symptoms in their patients. "This study is just a first step on the pathway to precision medicine in our field," she says.

Richard Friedman, a professor of clinical psychiatry at Weill Cornell Medical College, considers the goal of the McLean researchers laudable. But he notes that the road ahead remains challenging and warns that the history of psychology is filled with "objective assessments" for a particular diagnosis or state of mind that never lived up to their hype. Friedman cites the case of lie-detector tests, in which false positives and false negatives abound.

While a brain-based test that could diagnose dissociative symptoms is not likely anytime soon, research on neurobiological explanations show the controversy over forgetting and remembering traumatic memories is far from settled.

The Invisible Victims of Traumatic Brain Injury

By Anne P. DePrince and Kim Gorgens

Thousands of athletes returned to high school, college and professional football fields this fall, renewing discussions about the risk for and potentially devastating consequences of traumatic brain injuries (TBI) in contact sports. However, an even larger population of people affected by TBI will continue to go unrecognized and undiagnosed: women who are victims of domestic violence.

One in seven women has been injured by an intimate partner. Among women experiencing domestic violence, a handful of research teams across the U.S. have now documented alarming rates of head injuries, with studies suggesting that as many as 90 percent of women seeking emergency or shelter services for domestic violence report have had them.

Traumatic brain injuries occur when a blow to the head interrupts normal brain functioning. Those disruptions can include loss of consciousness, memory problems for the injury, muscle weakness and blurred vision. TBIs can range from mild to moderate or severe; most people experiencing mild TBIs won't have lasting symptoms. However, more serious and repeated TBIs can lead to serious and costly problems involving physical health; attention and memory; depression; suicidality; and even dementing diseases later in life.

Because of the serious problems linked with repeated TBIs, researchers and journalists have focused on groups likely to experience multiple head injuries, such as athletes playing contact sports and combat veterans. Like football players, victims of domestic violence often suffer from brain trauma—but with much less attention.

In research published by one of us (DePrince) with Kelly Gagnon, we interviewed more than 200 Colorado women following police reports of domestic violence. The incidents varied in severity; some cases involved violations of protection orders where there were no physical injuries, while others involved serious physical injury. More than one in 10 women described being hit in the head or losing consciousness during the most recent domestic violence incident. That number went up to 20 percent when we included domestic violence incidents that occurred in the previous six months.

Lifetime rates were even higher: 80 percent of women reported a head injury in their lifetimes. More than half of those met screening criteria for a mild TBI because the head injury involved a change in consciousness or a period of being dazed and confused.

Domestic violence did not cause all of those head injuries. Some were caused by child abuse or other kinds of assault. Others were the result of accidents. This raises the intriguing question of whether persistent TBI symptoms, regardless of their cause, increase women's risk of being victimized. For example, abusers might target women experiencing problems with attention, memory or depressive thinking that make them vulnerable.

We also don't know much about the frequency of head injuries among women in chronically violent relationships. Like football players, some women may be exposed to regular blows to the head, increasing their risk for persistent cognitive and emotional problems as well as dementing diseases down the road.

Even in the short term, TBI-related symptoms can have serious, real-world consequences for women trying to get help after domestic violence. These women commonly need help from multiple sources, including police; legal services; and medical and counseling professionals. Attention and memory problems, as well as depression symptoms, can make it difficult or impossible to figure out whom to contact and where to go, and also to schedule visits and remember complex instructions.

To answer these crucial questions of how TBI increases the risk of being abused, and what short- or long-term consequences this might have, we have to start paying attention to domestic violence and TBI to the same degree that we have attended to TBI in contact sports and combat. A 2015 report to Congress by the Centers for Disease Control and Prevention titled "Traumatic Brain Injury in the United States: Epidemiology and Rehabilitation," for example, did not even mention domestic violence.

Researchers, policymakers, and the public have been slow to consider TBI in the context of domestic violence. Women surviving domestic violence need us to act quickly to understand the scope of this public health problem and to design effective interventions. Their lives depend on it.

This article was published in Scientific American's *former blog network and reflects the views of the author, not necessarily those of* Scientific American.

About the Authors

Anne DePrince is department chair and professor of psychology at the University of Denver.

Kim Gorgens is a clinical professor in the Graduate School of Professional Psychology at the University of Denver.

Elon Musk's Secretive Brain Tech Company Debuts a Sophisticated Neural Implant

By Tanya Lewis and Gary Stix

L ate on Tuesday evening, Elon Musk, the charismatic and eccentric CEO of SpaceX and Tesla, took to the stage at the California Academy of Sciences to make a big announcement. This time, he was not unveiling a new rocket or electric car but a system for recording the activity of thousands of neurons in the brain. With typical panache, Musk talked about putting this technology into a human brain by as early as next year.

The work is the product of Neuralink, a company Musk founded in 2016 to develop a high-bandwidth, implantable brain-computer interface (BCI). He says the initial goal is to enable people with quadriplegia to control a computer or smartphone using just their thoughts. But Musk's vision is much more ambitious than that: he seeks to enable humans to "merge" with AI, giving people superhuman intelligence—an objective that is much more hype than an actual plan for new technology development.

On a more practical note, "the goal is to record from and stimulate [signals called] spikes in neurons" with an order of magnitude more bandwidth than what has been done to date and to have it be safe, Musk said at Tuesday's event, which was livestreamed.

The system unveiled last night was a long way from Musk's sci-fi vision. But it was nonetheless marked an impressive technical development. The team says it has now developed arrays with a very large number of "channels"—up to 3,072 flexible electrodes—which can be implanted in the brain's outer layer, or cortex, using a surgical robot (a version of which was described as a "sewing machine" in a preprint paper posted on bioRxiv earlier this year). The electrodes are packaged in a small, implantable device containing custom-built integrated circuits, which connects to a USB port outside the brain (the team hopes to ultimately make the port wireless). Neuralink also intends to have the electrodes write signals back into the brain to provide sensory feedback in the form of touch or of visual stimulation of the retina in a blind person. The company reported some initial results of its neural interface in rats in a white paper it made public, and it is currently doing experiments in monkeys at the University of California, Davis. None of this research has been peer-reviewed.

"More work in this area is great, and I think it's fantastic that they're giving this attention," says Ken Shepard, a professor of electrical and biomedical engineering at Columbia University, who is part of a Defense Advanced Research Projects Agency initiative to develop a flexible, implantable wireless chip that uses electrodes on the surface of the brain to record up to a million neurons. Neuralink is focused on three themes that will be important to any future brain-computer interface technology, Shepard says: flexible materials for the electrodes, miniaturization of the electronics with integrated circuit technology and fully wireless interaction with outside devices. "They have made significant progress in the first two," he says. But he adds that the challenges are going to be shrinking the electrical connections between the integrated circuits and the probes and incorporating many more electrodes without significantly increasing the size of the device. "The other big challenge is regulatory," he says, noting the use of penetrating electrodes of this scale in humans is going to face significant hurdles from the U.S. Food and Drug Administration.

One of the big problems with existing electrodes is that they can damage vasculature when the brain moves as it does with each breath and heartbeat. The new device aims to get around this problem by using a small but rigid needle that inserts the flexible, polymer-based electrode "threads"—each a tenth the width of a human hair—into the cortex, taking care to avoid veins or arteries on the way in.

Perhaps the gold standard in neural recording for BCI research is the Utah Array, which consists of a rigid grid of up to 128 electrode channels. This array has been successfully used in a number of BCIs, including the BrainGate device developed by researchers at Brown University and their colleagues. But it also causes a tissue response that can lead to scarring of tissue composed of glia (the brain's support cells), which may interfere with the quality of recorded signals or cause damage to brain cells. Another successful design is the Neuropixel, a probe developed by researchers at the Howard Hughes Medical Institute and their colleagues that consists of nearly 1,000 recording sites on a single tip, or shank, which can record from more than 500 neurons in the brains of mice. Developing tools for such high-density neural recording was one of the goals of the Obama administration's BRAIN Initiative.

Leigh Hochberg, a professor at Brown University and one of the leaders of the BrainGate team, calls the Neuralink system "a novel and exciting" neurotechnology. "Given the great potential that intracortical brain-computer interfaces have to restore neurologic function for people with spinal cord injury, stroke, [amyotrophic lateral sclerosis], traumatic brain injury, or other diseases or injuries of the nervous system, I'm excited to see how [the company will] be translating [its] system toward initial clinical studies," adds Hochberg, who is also a neurologist at Massachusetts General Hospital and the Providence VA Medical Center.

Neuralink claims its system can record from about 1,500 or 3,000 electrodes, depending on the version of the device being tested. The company asserts that because its electrodes are much thinner and more flexible, they are less likely to cause tissue damage. At the event, Musk said the reason for going with an invasive BCI—rather than one that detects neural signals outside the brain, such as electroencephalography—is that the company wants to record signals from individual neurons. "Everything we see, perceive or think are action potentials, or spikes," he said. Musk noted that the ultimate goal is to make Neuralink's device available to anyone, not just those with serious neurological illnesses, and to have it implanted in a minimally invasive procedure akin to LASIK eye surgery—though experts say such an achievement is a long way off.

The company hopes to begin its first human trial next year, the team said last night. This is an extremely ambitious target, given it still needs to obtain the necessary approval from the FDA, however.

Others in the field were gratified to get some transparency from a company that has shrouded itself in secrecy over the past few years. "Everyone is really appreciative that Elon has thrown his weight behind BCIs and brought visibility to the field," says Matt Angle, founder and CEO of Paradromics—a firm that is also developing high-data-rate brain-computer interfaces—who is also part of the DARPA project. Angle is not as surprised by the technical developments, saying the achievements build on previous work by Neuralink senior scientist Philip "Flip" Sabes and bioengineer Timothy Hanson while they were both at the University of California, San Francisco. He notes that a challenge of such polymer-based electrodes is that they do not last as long as other inorganic materials when subjected to harsh conditions of the body. But he thinks Neuralink's microfabrication expert Vanessa Tolosa and her team have made some impressive progress in materials science. Overall, Angle says, "I saw the most significant part of the announcement being [a willingness to] open up and engage with the community."

About the Authors

Tanya Lewis is a senior editor covering health and medicine at Scientific American. *She writes and edits stories for the website and print magazine on topics ranging from COVID to organ transplants. She also co-hosts* Your Health, Quickly *on Scientific American's podcast* Science, Quickly *and writes* Scientific American's *weekly* Health & Biology *newsletter. She has held a number of positions over her seven years at* Scientific American, *including health editor, assistant news editor and associate editor at* Scientific American Mind. *Previously, she has written for outlets that include* Insider, Wired, Science News, *and others. She has a degree in biomedical engineering from Brown University and one in science communication from the University of California, Santa Cruz.*

Gary Stix, Scientific American's *neuroscience and psychology editor, commissions, edits and reports on emerging advances and technologies that have propelled brain science to the forefront of the biological sciences. Developments chronicled in dozens of cover stories, feature articles and news stories, document ground-breaking neuroimaging techniques that reveal what happens in the brain while you are immersed in thought; the arrival of brain implants that alleviate mood disorders like depression; lab-made brains; psychological resilience; meditation; the intricacies of sleep; the new era for psychedelic drugs and artificial intelligence and growing insights leading to an understanding of our conscious selves. Before taking over the neuroscience beat, Stix, as* Scientific American's *special projects editor, oversaw the magazine's annual single-topic special issues, conceiving of and producing issues on Einstein, Darwin, climate change, nanotechnology and the nature of time. The issue he edited on time won a National Magazine Award. Besides mind and brain coverage, Stix has edited or written cover stories on Wall Street quants, building the world's tallest building, Olympic training methods, molecular electronics, what makes us human and the things you should and should not eat. Stix started a monthly column, Working Knowledge, that gave the reader a peek at the design and function of common technologies, from polygraph machines to Velcro. It eventually became the magazine's Graphic Science column. He also initiated a column on patents and intellectual property and another on the genesis of the ingenious ideas underlying new technologies in fields like electronics and biotechnology. Stix is the author with his wife, Miriam Lacob, of a technology primer called* Who Gives a Gigabyte: A Survival Guide to the Technologically Perplexed *(John Wiley & Sons, 1999).*

New Brain Implant Turns Visualized Letters into Text

By Bret Stetka

W hen you move, sense, speak, or do just about anything, your brain generates a specific corresponding pattern of electrical activity. For decades, scientists have run these impulses through machines to better understand brain diseases and help people with disabilities. Brain-computer interfaces (BCIs) under development can restore movement in some who have paralysis, and researchers are working on BCIs to treat neurological and psychiatric disorders.

The next frontier in BCIs, however, may be something more like writing a text message. A new study in *Nature* describes a brain implant that could let individuals with impaired limb movement create text using the mind—no hands needed.

For their study, the researchers coupled artificial-intelligence software with electrodes implanted in the brain of a man with full-body paralysis. He was asked to imagine himself writing by hand, and the BCI transformed his visualized letters and words into text on a computer screen. Such technology could potentially benefit millions of people worldwide who cannot type or speak because of impaired limbs or vocal muscles.

Previous work by Krishna V. Shenoy of Stanford University, a co-senior author on the study, had helped analyze neural patterns associated with speech. His software also decoded imagined arm movements, so that those with paralysis could move a cursor around an on-screen keyboard to select and type letters. But this technique let people generate just 40 characters per minute, far lower than the average keyboard typing speed of roughly 190. The researchers' new work sped up communication speed by using imagined handwriting. Their technique allowed the study subject, who was 65 years old at the time, to mentally type 90 characters per minute. That rate approaches the average for most senior texters, who can typically type about 115 characters per minute on a phone.

"This line of work could help restore communication in people who are severely paralyzed, or 'locked-in,'" says Frank Willett, lead author of the paper and a research scientist at Stanford's Neural Prosthetics Translational Laboratory. "It should help people express themselves and share their thoughts; it's very exciting."

The study participant had suffered a spinal cord injury in 2007, losing most movement below his neck. In 2016 Stanford neurosurgeon Jaimie Henderson, co-senior author of the paper, implanted two small BCI chips into the man's brain. Each chip had 100 electrodes to sense neuron activity. They were implanted in a region of the motor cortex that controls hand and arm movements, letting the researchers profile brain-activity patterns associated with written language.

"This study is an important and clear advance for intracortical brain-computer interfaces," says University of Washington bioengineer Amy L. Orsborn, who was not involved in the research. "One obvious reason why is because they achieved a huge leap in performance on a challenging but important task like typing. It's also the most significant demonstration to date of leveraging established tools in machine learning, like predictive language models, to improve BCIs."

Mijail D. Serruya, a neurologist at Thomas Jefferson University, who studies BCIs in stroke recovery but was not involved in the new study, is intrigued by the work. "I saw this research initially presented ... in 2019 and think it's great," he says. "I think it clearly shows that fine-motor trajectories can be decoded from neocortical activity."

Serruya adds that his own research could align with Willett's in helping those who have suffered brain trauma or a stroke. "We have shown that motor-control signals can be decoded [following a stroke], implying that some of the decoding approaches developed by Willett might have applications beyond people with spinal cord injury," he says.

Yet Serruya also has a question about the new research, a hesitation he says he posed to Willett a few years ago: while restoring communication via written letters is intuitive, it may not be the most efficient means of doing so.

"Why not teach the person a new language based on simpler elementary gestures, similar to stenography chords or sign language?" Serruya asks. "This could both boost the speed of communication and, crucially, decrease the mental effort and attention needed."

For now, Willett is focused on mentally decoding more familiar forms of communication—and he wants to repeat the typing experiment, involving more people with paralysis. Translating the brain's control over handwriting may be a significant first step in restoring communication skills, he says. But decoding actual speech—by analyzing what someone intends to say—is still a major challenge facing researchers, given that individuals generate speech more quickly than they write or type.

"It's been a hard problem to decode speech with enough accuracy and vocabulary size to allow people to have a general conversation. There's a much higher signal-to-noise ratio, so it's harder to translate to the computer," Willett says. "But we're now excited that we can decode handwriting very accurately. Each letter evokes a very different pattern of neural activity."

As for when text-and-speech-decoding technology might be available to the public, Willett is cautiously optimistic. "It's hard to predict when our method will be translated into a real device that anyone can buy," he says. "There are companies working on implantable BCI devices now, but you never know when someone will succeed in translating it. We hope it's within years, not decades!"

About the Author

Bret Stetka was a writer based in New York City and editorial director of Medscape Neurology (a subsidiary of WebMD). His work has appeared in Wired, NPR and the Atlantic. He graduated from the University of Virginia School of Medicine in 2005. Stetka died in 2022.

GLOSSARY

action potential A rapid change in electrical charge in a nerve cell.

amygdala A region of the brain, near its center, associated with fear and other emotions.

anecdote A brief real story used to illustrate a point.

axon A component of a nerve cell that carries electrical impulses to other cells. Axons can vary in length.

bolster To give strength, support, or evidence to something.

cerebral cortex The outer layer of the brain, typically associated with thinking, learning, and problem-solving.

chagrin Annoyance or mild distress at having been proven wrong.

cognition The mental process of perceiving, reflecting and understanding.

elusive The property of being difficult to locate or understand.

episodic memory Memory of an individual's life experience that can be determined with a particular place or time.

firing rate The number of action potentials in a given neuron over time.

flatline Medical term for the death (or near-death) experience, during which vital signs on medical equipment drop.

gray matter Substance of the outer layers of the brain, comprising primarily nerve cell bodies and their synapses.

hippocampus A brain structure that plays a significant role in forming memories.

homogeneous Of the same type or alike, rather than varied and different.

hype Significant publicity or promotion for something.

motor cortex The region of the brain associated with physical movements.

myelin A layer of insulation around nerve axons. The health of myelin layers is associated with effective learning.

neuron A cell, prominent in the brain, which sends and receives electrical impulses.

parse To analyze and determine how components of something fit together.

stigma Social dishonor for a specific physical or other feature.

symptom A health characteristic that is considered a sign of one or more diseases.

synapse An electrical transmission point between a nerve cell and another cell.

white matter Substance of the inner layers of the brain, comprising primarily nerve cell axons and their myelin sheaths.

FURTHER INFORMATION

"BRAIN 2025: A Scientific Vision," The BRAIN Initiative. https://braininitiative.nih.gov/vision/nih-brain-initiative-reports/brain-2025-scientific-vision.

"Brain Anatomy and How the Brain Works," Johns Hopkins Medicine. https://www.hopkinsmedicine.org/health/conditions-and-diseases/anatomy-of-the-brain.

Dosenbach, Nico U.F. "How Our Team Overturned the 90-Year-Old Metaphor of a 'Little Man' in the Brain Who Controls Movement," *Scientific American*, April 21, 2023. https://www.scientificamerican.com/article/how-our-team-overturned-the-90-year-old-metaphor-of-a-little-man-in-the-brain-who-controls-movement1/.

Koch, Christof. "What Is Consciousness?," *Scientific American*, June 1, 2018. https://www.scientificamerican.com/article/what-is-consciousness/.

Leffer, Lauren. "Worm Brains, Decoded like Never Before, Could Shed Light on Our Own Mind," *Scientific American*, August 21, 2023. https://www.scientificamerican.com/article/worm-brains-decoded-like-never-before-could-shed-light-on-our-own-mind/.

Makin, Tamar, and John Krakauer. "The Brain Isn't as Adaptable as Some Neuroscientists Claim," *Scientific American*, November 21, 2023, https://www.scientificamerican.com/article/the-brain-isnt-as-adaptable-as-some-neuroscientists-claim/.

Olagunju, Abdulrahman. "Cells Deep in Your Brain Place Time Stamps on Memories," *Scientific American*, December 29, 2021. https://www.scientificamerican.com/article/cells-deep-in-your-brain-place-time-stamps-on-memories/.

Rojahn, Susan. "Tools Used for Human Research," BrainFacts.org. https://www.brainfacts.org/in-the-lab/tools-and-techniques/2023/tools-used-for-human-research-030923.

CITATIONS

1.1 The Father of Modern Neuroscience Discovered the Basic Unit of the Nervous System by Benjamin Ehrlich (April 1 2022); 1.2 The Hidden Brain by R. Douglas Fields (May 1, 2011); 1.3 Newfound Hybrid Brain Cells Send Signals like Neurons Do by Simon Makin (December 1, 2023); 2.1 A Challenge to the Textbooks on How We Learn about Our Surroundings by Gary Stix (September 20, 2017); 2.2 Emotion Selectively Distorts Our Recollections by Ingfei Chen (January 1, 2012); 2.3 Deeper Insights Emerge into How Memories Form by R. Douglas Fields (November 18, 2019); 3.1 Controlling the Brain With Light by Karl Deisseroth (November 1, 2010); 3.2 A Cell Atlas Reveals the Biodiversity inside Our Head by Christof Koch, Ed S. Lein & Hongkui Zeng (October 6, 2021); 3.3 "Mini Brains" Are Not like the Real Thing by Karen Weintraub (January 30, 2020); 3.4 The Fading Dream of the Computer Brain by Noah Hutton (April 29, 2021); 4.1 How Our Brain Preserves Our Sense of Self by Robert Martone (December 21, 2021); 4.2 A 25-Year-Old Bet about Consciousness Has Finally Been Settled by John Horgan (June 26, 2023); 4.3 Some Patients Who 'Died' but Survived Report Lucid 'Near-Death Experiences,' a New Study Shows by Rachel Nuwer (September 14, 2023); 4.4 How the Mind Emerges from the Brain's Complex Networks by Max Bertolero & Dani S. Bassett (July 1, 2019); 5.1 What Makes Our Brains Special? by Diana Kwon (November 24, 2015); 5.2 Bird Brains Have as Many Neurons as Some Primates by Sara Chodosh (June 16, 2016); 5.3 The Genius of Pinheads: When Little Brains Rule by Erik Vance (March 28, 2017); 5.4 Cetaceans' Big Brains Are Linked to Their Rich Social Life by Diana Kwon & Amanda Montañez (November 24, 2017); 6.1 Five Types of Research, Underexplored until Recently, Could Produce Alzheimer's Treatments by Kenneth S. Kosik (May 1, 2020); 6.2 New Research Points to Causes for Brain Disorders with No Obvious Injury by Z Paige L'Erario (March 31, 2023); 6.3 Forgotten Memories of Traumatic Events Get Some Backing from Brain-Imaging Studies by Joshua Kendall (April 6, 2021); 6.4 The Invisible Victims of Traumatic Brain Injury by Anne P. DePrince & Kim Gorgens (November 13, 2019); 6.5 Elon Musk's Secretive Brain Tech Company Debuts a Sophisticated Neural Implant by Tanya Lewis & Gary Stix (July 17, 2019); 6.6 New Brain Implant Turns Visualized Letters into Text by Bret Stetka (May 12, 2021).

Each author biography was accurate at the time the article was originally published.

INDEX

A

aging, 16, 20–21, 39, 127, 129
amygdala, 35–36, 39–40, 43, 94, 134, 140
animal brains, 106–121
artificial intelligence, 76–77, 86–87, 94, 117–118, 141, 146, 151
astrocytes, 15, 17–19, 21–24, 26–27, 66
axon, 11, 16–20, 22, 30, 44–46, 63, 65–66, 115, 124

B

Bassett, Dani S., 93–104
Bertolero, Max, 93–104
brain-computer interface, 146–153
brain size, 106, 108, 110–111, 113–119

C

cerebral cortex, 13, 21, 23, 36, 43, 47–49, 63–64, 66–68, 72, 79–82, 87, 106, 140, 146–147, 152
Chen, Ingfei, 34–43
Chodosh, Sara, 110–112
consciousness/perception, 8–9, 23, 143–144
Crick, Francis, 51–52, 84, 87

D

death, 89–92
dementia, 16, 87, 143
  Alzheimer's disease, 20–21, 27, 61, 64, 70–71, 107, 122–132
  frontotemporal dementia, 64
dendrite, 16–17, 30–32, 63, 65, 124, 129
DePrince, Anne P., 143–145
disassociative amnesia, 138–142

E

Ehrlich, Benjamin, 8–14
electrical activity, 15–20, 29–30, 65, 67, 89–90, 93, 95, 123, 130–131, 134, 151
electrical therapy, 24, 51–62, 86, 94, 102
emotion, 23, 29, 34–43, 51, 62, 80–81, 94, 96–97, 99, 101, 131, 140
ethics, 61–62, 72, 75, 77
evolution, 9, 63, 76, 82, 91, 97, 102–103, 106, 111–112, 115, 119–120
executive function, 81, 97, 100, 140

F

Fields, R. Douglas, 15–25, 44–49

G

genetics, 22–23, 51–63, 65–68, 70–72, 76, 94, 104, 107–108, 122, 126–130

glia, 15–24, 26, 44, 66, 72, 107–108, 148

global workspace theory, 87–88

Gorgens, Kim, 143–145

H

Haller's rule, 113–117

hippocampus, 18, 21, 26, 30–32, 36, 40, 42–43, 47–49, 82

Horgan, John, 84–88

Hutton, Noah, 74–77

I

immune system, 124, 128–129

injury, 16, 20–22, 80–81, 91, 103, 123, 128–129, 131, 134, 141, 143–145, 148, 152

integrated information theory, 85–88

K

Kendall, Joshua, 138–142

Kensinger, Elizabeth A., 38–40

Koch, Christof, 63–69, 84–88

Kosik, Kenneth S., 122–132

Kriegstein, Arnold, 70–73

Kwon, Diana, 106–109, 119–120

L

language, 106, 152–153

learning/intelligence, 15, 19, 29–32, 35, 44–46, 48–49, 79, 93, 97, 100, 110–111, 116, 118

Lein, Ed S., 63–69, 108

L'Erario, Z Paige, 133–137

Lewis, Tanya, 146–150

M

Magee, Jeffrey, 30–32

Markram, Henry, 74–77

Mather, Mara, 38–40

memory, 15, 18–19, 26–27, 29–32, 34–49, 51, 62, 64, 79–82, 93, 96–99, 116, 129–131, 138–143

mental illness, 16, 20, 58, 72, 74, 100, 103, 109
  anxiety, 39, 41
  depression, 22–24, 41, 51, 53, 59, 94, 101–102, 143
  obsessive-compulsive disorder, 22
  post-traumatic stress disorder, 41, 47, 139–141
  schizophrenia, 22–24, 51, 53, 60, 70, 101
  suicide, 143

microglia, 16, 20–22, 66, 124, 128–130

Musk, Elon, 74, 146–150

myelin, 6, 11, 19–20, 22–23, 44–49

N

nervous system, 9–15, 53, 63–64, 138, 148
Nestor, Michael, 71–73
Neuralink, 74, 146–150
neurological disorders, 15–16, 20–23, 58, 64, 72, 74, 109
  amyotrophic lateral sclerosis, 64, 133, 148
  autism, 60, 70, 72, 77
  epilepsy, 24, 27, 64
  functional neurological disorder, 133–137
  multiple sclerosis, 22, 44, 133
  Parkinson's disease, 27, 53, 59–60, 133
  stroke, 103, 135, 148, 152
  Tourette's syndrome, 135
neurotransmitter, 15, 17–20, 23–24, 26, 51, 55, 130
Nuwer, Rachel, 89–92

O

oligodendrocyte, 16, 19, 22, 44–45, 66
optogenetics, 51–62, 86, 130

P

Parnia, Sam, 89–92
plasticity, 14, 29, 31–32, 108
prescription drugs, 23, 55, 58, 61–62, 72, 94, 122, 125

R

Ramón y Cajal, Santiago, 8–14, 63

S

sense of self, 79–83, 116
sleep/dreaming, 24, 40–41, 46–48, 53, 87, 90, 98, 131
spinal cord, 64, 66–67, 152
Stetka, Bret, 151–153
Stix, Gary, 29–33, 146–150
substance abuse, 59, 98
synapse, 15–19, 23, 30, 32, 44, 46, 49, 76, 93, 124–125, 130

T

thalamus, 64, 67

V

Vance, Erik, 113–118

W

Walker, Matthew P., 40–41
Weintraub, Karen, 70–73

Z

Zeng, Hongkui, 63–69
Zhang, Feng, 55–56